QUALITY

VALUE

BANKING

Effective Management Systems That Increase Earnings, Lower Costs, and Provide Competitive Customer Service

JANET L. GRAY

THOMAS W. HARVEY

John Wiley & Sons, Inc.

New York / Chichester / Brisbane / Toronto / Singapore

To Peter, Jessica, and Sarah,
who agreed on my direction   *—J.L.G.*

To Barbara, for her love, support, and constant
encouragement, and to Doug, who continues
to make his dad very proud   *—T.W.H.*

Copyright © 1992 by Janet L. Gray and Thomas W. Harvey
Published by John Wiley & Sons, Inc.
All rights reserved. Published simultaneously in Canada.

Library of Congress Cataloging-in-Publication Data

Gray, Janet L.
    Quality value banking : effective management systems that increase earnings, lower costs, and provide competitive customer service / by Janet L. Gray, Thomas W. Harvey.
      p. cm.
    Includes index.
    ISBN 0-471-55009-4
    1. Bank management—Quality control. 2. Quality of products.
3. Banks and banking—Customer services. I. Harvey, Thomas W.
II. Title.
HG1616.G73 1992
332.1'068—dc20   92-1283

Printed in the United States of America
10 9 8 7 6 5 4 3 2 1

Contents

Acknowledgments   v

1 / The Foundation of Quality Value Banking   1

2 / The Banker's World Has Changed   22

3 / Quality Improvement Is the Answer   53

4 / The Quality Value Engineering (QVE) Approach   78

5 / Getting Organized   112

6 / How to Implement Quality Value Engineering   140

7 / Value Creation Dialogues   159

8 / The Malcolm Baldrige National Quality Award   181

9 / The Beginning   208

Glossary   225

Index   229

Acknowledgments

Quality Value Banking is the result of several years of studying banks. It came about when we realized the effect that organization structure and environment have on service quality levels and how that can be traced to the bank's financial statements.

In 1988, when we first heard that *30 percent of what the bank does is related to doing things wrong or to things that don't have to be done at all*, we may not have realized how profound that statement was. We were skeptical of it, guided by traditional thinking, but then Leonard L. Berry of Texas A&M University made it very clear to us that quality service can be a profit strategy.

Berry's work with Valarie Zeithaml, A. Parasuraman, Carter Brown, and David Bennett triggered our thinking about improving processes to provide services according to customer expectations. Based on that, we developed Quality Value Engineering, a process by which banks can improve themselves and the service they provide to their customers. We are indebted to them all for their pioneering work.

Improving service quality depends on data about the perceptions and expectations of customers and then acting on that information to make the enhancements. But it is also a matter of structure, culture, and attitude that requires the bank to be organized and managed with a focus that is directly on the customer. We are thankful for the significant contributions of W. Edwards Deming, Joseph Juran, Armand Feigenbaum, Philip Crosby, Tom Peters, and many others who initiated, and now continue, the mission of improving the quality of our goods and services. We also appreciate the publication of *The Fifth Discipline*, by Peter Senge, which really taught us the value of systems thinking.

Our objective in *Quality Value Banking* is to link all of these disciplines into one process that will teach bankers and other professionals how to help themselves improve financially. To do so requires an understanding of these linkages and then a passion for correcting the root causes of service quality problems wherever they may be found throughout the organization.

We could not have written *Quality Value Banking* without a lot of help. As such, we would like to acknowledge and thank the many people whom we interviewed during the past year. We are grateful for your willingness to share your views, anecdotes, and opinions with us:

Chuck Aubrey—Senior Vice President, BancOne Corporation
Doug Bannerman—Senior Vice President, National City Corporation
Len Barker—Senior Vice President, Society Corporation
Charles Berkey—Senior Vice President, Ameritrust Co.
David Bowers, Ph.D.—Weatherhead School of Management, Case Western Reserve University
Judy Brooks—Vice President, J. P. Morgan & Co.
Wayne Cassatt, Ph.D.—Deputy Director, Malcolm Baldrige National Quality Award
Bonnie Cornell—Partner, Royal Trust Bank (Can.)
Bill Deedrick—former Cashier, Union Commerce Bank
Shane Flynn—Executive Vice President, MBNA America
John Gonas—Senior Vice President, Huntington National Bank
Bruce Hammonds—Vice Chairman, MBNA America
Dave Hanick—Senior Vice President, National City Bank
Jack Hewes—Executive Vice President, MBNA America
Andy Hewitt—Vice President, Huntington National Bank
Rick Hyde—Executive Vice President, Ameritrust Co.
Margaret Kerns—Chief Quality Officer, Bank One—Dayton
John Kinman—Executive Vice President, U.S. Bancorp
Bob Lias—Vice President, Bank One—Cleveland
Earl Livengood—Corporate Auditor, U.S. Bancorp
Chuck Long—Vice President, U.S. Bancorp
Greg Lunde—President, PolyCentric Strategies, Inc.
Janine Marrone—Executive Vice President, MBNA America
Maureen McKernan—Vice President, MBNA America
Cathy Mitchell—Vice President, National City Bank
Judy Moshberger—Human Resources, U.S. Bancorp
Jennifer Myhre—Director of Quality Performance, American Savings Bank
Connie Rawlings—Assistant Vice President, U.S. Bancorp

Richard Paegelow—Vice President, First Interstate Bank of California
Mike Quigley—Vice President, Society Corporation
Lou Raffis—Vice President, Society Corporation
Ann Rothgeb—Office of Quality Programs, National Institute of Standards and Technology
Dale Ruby—Senior Vice President, Security Pacific National Bank
Dave Sanders—Vice President, National City Bank
Sal Sarrantino—President, California Research Corporation
Craig Schroeder—Vice President, MBNA America
Bernie Stothard—Vice President, Lorain National Bank
Dan Sullivan—Controller, U.S. Bancorp
Mike Trigg—Senior Vice President, Society Corporation
Dave Vernon—President, Summit Bank
Bob Vezina—Senior Vice President, First Tennessee National Bank
Rod White—Vice President, First Tennessee National Bank

We would also like to express our thanks to those who have provided all kinds of support for us during the writing of *Quality Value Banking:*

Our parents, Nancy & Ted Gray and Mary & Bob Harvey
Our wonderful travel agent, Candace LeVine of Novelty Travel
Bill Work, TradeWeek
Our agent, Jeff Herman
Our editor, Wendy Grau
Our support staff at John Wiley & Sons
The Board of Directors of the Southern California chapter of the Institute of Management Consultants, especially its Vice President David Gering of The Write Source
The Board of Directors of the National Association for Bank Cost and Management Accounting, especially Jim Ricordati of First Chicago, Art Grossman of State Street Bank and Trust, and Joe Gagliano of Marine Midland
Dr. Scott Cowen, Dr. J. B. Silvers, and Dr. Ron Fry of the Weatherhead School of Management and their teachings about value creation
David Carroll Johnson
Jack Kluznik, Curt Oliver, and the rest of the running club at the Cleveland Athletic Club
Ernie DuRoss
Scott Lange, and
Steve Harvey

And, special thanks to Bill Schrauth, Dawn Drewnowski, the Quality Excellence Council, the Employee Communication and Mortgage Lending Value Creation teams, and everyone else at The Savings Bank of Utica, (N.Y.).

Los Angeles, California   Janet Gray
Chagrin Falls, Ohio   Tom Harvey
February, 1992

Chapter 1

The Foundation of Quality Value Banking

The thesis of this book is simple, and the reader need not wait until Chapter 4 or 5 to find out what it is: The foundation of quality in banks and in any company is organization structure. If an institution is not organized for quality, it will not have it. It is a necessary, although not sufficient, condition for excellence in service, products, and processes. The right structure will not guarantee success, but the wrong structure will surely prevent it. Banks, for the most part, have the wrong structure.

The quality improvement methodology for banks presented in this book, Quality Value Engineering, exploits this relationship of structure to quality as no method that has gone before. Other quality improvement programs acknowledge structure, some more than others, but no other process gets to the root causes of poor quality, the causes that rest in the way work, people, units, and missions are organized. Once the root causes are discovered and addressed, then and only then can the quality improvement process begin. Changing processes can change systems, but it all gets back to people and individual jobs, individual behaviors. If these aren't "fixed," other fixes will be temporary and short-term at best, if not a complete waste of time.

This opening chapter shows why organization structure is the sine qua non of excellent quality and continual quality improvement. It presents the relationships between it and organizational culture or environment, and service quality issues (later this book will take the relationship a step farther and relate service quality to increased profitability and other performance improvements). It demonstrates the ways in which poor structure negatively affects quality improvement attempts. Finally, it teaches organization structure assessment and provides some benchmarks to which to compare various structural statistics.

THE HISTORY OF ORGANIZATION STRUCTURE

In order to provide a common language, it will be useful to define "organization structure." It is commonly and usefully thought of as the result of *dividing* and *coordinating* work. It is comprised of two major components: work design, or the definition of tasks, responsibilities, and expected results of various work units; and the management structure, or the coordinating mechanism whose purpose is to oversee the work and ensure its execution in synchronization with the entity's ruling mission.

The most widely known form of organization structure is based on the "military model." The military, along with the church, is probably the oldest form of organization as well as the most successful. Its pyramidal form is the one that most of us think of when we think of organization structure, and that shape is a consequence of several "rules" that are embodied in the structure itself.

The military model is predicated on two fundamental and seemingly conflicting tenets: divide and conquer, and unity of command. Organizational goals are broken down into their component tasks and parceled out to workers and specialists who actually perform the work. The coordinating mechanism in the military model is "control" or "authority," so supervisors and managers are placed above these workers in various intervals to oversee them. Each worker, according to the unity of command rule, must have one and only one manager, and each manager has a finite "span of control," or number of people that he or she can effectively oversee. As the number of first-level managers increases, a second layer of management must be installed to oversee it. Thus, levels of management are created that follow a "chain of command" up to the supreme commander. Each succeeding level requires fewer managers; hence the pyramid shape.

The military model has been successful for a long, long time, although there are indications that even the military may be restructuring it. There are good reasons for its success. It is the perfect structure for an uneducated and relatively unskilled workforce. It is very effective in a stable environment that is more or less predictable. Perhaps most important, it is self-perpetuating. All those management slots, combined with the inviolable chain of command, create an expectation in the minds of those inhabiting the slots below, namely, that as slots become vacant, there is an opportunity for advancement through the ranks. Furthermore, there is only one avenue of advancement, and that is through the established structure.

This expectation serves two purposes. First, it motivates those hoping to advance to perform well. Second, it controls them, by tacitly encouraging them to follow the successful patterns of their predecessors. In the stable environment in which this structure thrives, the chain of command and narrow vision of all but the top executives ensure a controlled, smoothly functioning organization.

This basic pattern of organization has shaped American business entities since the Industrial Revolution. It is not the only model of organization. The "matrix" form of organization, which explicitly breaks the "unity of command" rule, was a highly popular though very difficult form of organization in the 1980s. Most companies, particularly banks, that tried to implement matrix management have reverted to the military model, citing the confusion and psychological barriers that result from serving two masters.

Systems of compensation and other rewards have served to reinforce the military model. One of the most widely known compensation systems is the Hay point system. Although complex and comprehensive in nature, the Hay system has been too often simplistically interpreted to reward, by rating their jobs highly, managers with large staffs and budgets. This interpretation has encouraged empire-building and discouraged the pursuit of nonmanagerial careers. These dual impacts have resulted in excessive bureaucracy and unsupported overhead in many organizations.

BANKS' STRUCTURE

Have banks followed this pattern? Indeed they have. Banks epitomize the pyramidal military model and embody the characteristics and problems embedded in it.

Consider how the typical bank structures itself. At the top is the bank president; at the bottom are the workers—the tellers, the operations people, the loan officers, the staff employees such as credit review, finance, marketing, human resources, and legal. Over these workers a management structure develops. A branch manager and an operations manager are installed; the controller, credit officer, and personnel specialist are busy staffing themselves—maybe even "building empires" to enhance their job rating and thus their financial and nonfinancial rewards. A marketing specialist is employed; she builds her staff. The bank is successful and so another branch is opened, and another, and another—with more branch managers. The operations people are working overtime to keep up with transaction volume so a shift is added—and another manager. More specialists are added, more branches, more staff. The president can't keep track of it all and adds another layer of management.

Does this scenario, depicted in Figure 1.1, sound and look familiar? It should. This is how banks grow. This is how banks look. For years banks have relied on this structure to maintain control over a fiduciary charter that was highly respectable, responsible, and, most important, regulated. Since the 1930s

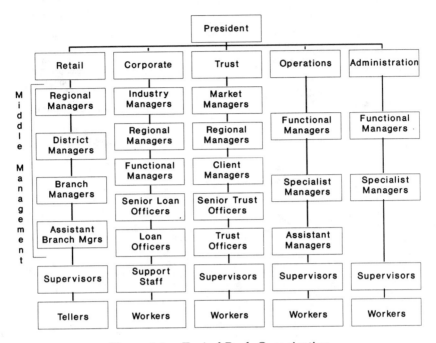

Figure 1.1. Typical Bank Organization

until recently, banks and savings and loans have had their financial province of deposit-taking and loan-making all to themselves, and since interest rates were fixed for them, profit margins were also fixed and highly satisfactory. Banks could hardly lose: They made approximately four cents for every dollar put on the books, and they were basically the only game in town. The environment was stable; regulation virtually guaranteed profits; banks continued to grow and grow.

The model in Figure 1.2 shows that the driving force in this scenario is the stable environment, characterized by interest ceilings resulting in fixed profit margins. Increasing customer volume caused profitability to go up and required significant additions to staff and branches. These measures enabled the banks to attract more customers, and the cycle perpetuated itself.

From the 1930s to the beginning of the 1970s this was the scenario. The pyramidal, military organization structure was

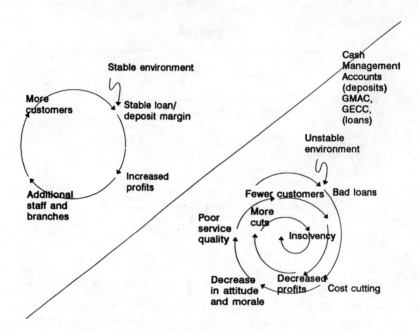

Figure 1.2. Cycle of Stability and the Downward Spiral

adequate for this environment, although arguably not the best one. There were three things wrong with it. First, the bank president was isolated from markets and customers. The president no longer received information directly from them, and was unable to plan the bank's direction according to their (changing) needs. Second, a large infrastructure (read overhead) was created. Even though technology was soon to render the ubiquitous branch system unnecessary and its staff redundant, the bank was saddled with rising fixed expenses of which it could not easily divest itself. Tradition alone dictated that it not do so. Third, the divisions of labor were driven by function or process, not by the customer. Banks were focused inward, not outward. They lost touch. All these factors created real problems for banks.

Starting in about 1973 the environment was anything but stable. Myriad forces began upsetting the cozy world of regulated banking. These forces fell into four major areas:

- *Economics.* In the United States and in the world at large recession was combining with rampant inflation to create a never-before-seen condition of "stagflation." The end of the Vietnam War, the oil crisis, and runaway interest rates contributed to extraordinarily turbulent economic conditions.

- *Deregulation.* Deregulation of both interest rates and competition progressed at a rapid rate. New competitors entered the field led by Merrill Lynch's cash management account and quickly followed by others. Banks began complaining about the uneven "playing field," and deregulation was pursued as the way to level it.

- *Technology.* Banks were investing in systems technology in a massive way. They had to; their new competitors were. Technology was the key to reducing costs, but required an enormous investment and caused a drain on earnings.

- *Geography.* De facto interstate banking was occurring throughout the country. Suddenly Citicorp and Bank of America were in each other's backyard, and in everyone else's, too. Furthermore, foreign banks were acquiring a greater interest in America's financial markets, including the Japanese, who had already wreaked havoc in such stalwart American industries as automobiles and steel.

Chapter 2 will present more information about the squeeze on profit margins and overall earnings these conditions put on the banks, and discuss some of the strategies banks pursued to deal with it. These strategies took time, however, both to develop and especially to implement, because banks simply weren't structured to cope with massive change: They were too big, too bureaucratic, too burdened with fixed overhead expenses.

Look again at the model in Figure 1.1. The bracketed area represents that maligned and infamous organization phenomenon known as the "middle management bulge." There almost certainly were too many middle managers—positions that existed to process information and communicate orders. But within those ranks lay the only chance that banks had to make positive and proactive changes in the way they did business.

At the lowest level, the worker level, jobs were highly specialized and highly controlled. Entry-level jobs in banks were neither prestigious nor highly paid, and the work design reflected that. There was little cross-training in those days, little room for advancement past first-level supervisor, and virtually no opportunity to understand, much less improve, operational processes. Workers were expected to do their jobs as quickly as possible. Legally mandated deadlines left no time for creative thinking.

At the senior levels, a different kind of force was felt. As executives rose toward the top, the pressure to conform became ever stronger. People tend to hire in their own image, and ambitious executives were increasingly adept at understanding what the chief liked, admired, and valued, and emulating it to the best of their ability. There was very little innovation and risk-taking at this level.

So middle managers were the only ones with the opportunity to do anything creative. Their jobs were fairly flexible, relative to the specialized workers below them. And they had not yet begun to feel the conforming pressures too heavily. They, and only they, had the requisite freedom from time and peer pressure to develop innovative responses to the challenges that were presenting themselves in the new financial environment.

But what happened? For the first time in history, white-collar professionals and middle managers took the big cuts when the big cost-cutting began. And with those cost reductions banks lost any chance they had to find a new way of doing business, because the survivors certainly weren't about to stick their necks out on new ideas. They hunkered down, did their jobs, kept their noses clean, and tried to stay as invisible as possible. The sad and ironic part of the whole messy process was that as much as 80 percent of the costs that were cut during this time probably came back in two years or less. (Some studies show that 125 percent of the costs will creep back over time, and not a very long time at that.)

TIME FOR A CHANGE

Now we are in the 1990s, heading for the new century. Things have settled down considerably since those turbulent days of the 1970s, leading to the merger and acquisition craze of the 1980s. Deregulation is incomplete but pervasive, and although there may be some reregulation, clearly things will not go back to the way they were before. Interstate banking is with us, even though Congress is lagging behind in making it official. The economy, though by no means robust, is fairly stable and may be heading up again. The banking industry, particularly the very large money center and regional banks, is consolidating itself. The days of hostile takeovers financed by junk bonds and other dubious instruments appear to be behind us.

Because the environment is relatively stable now, does that mean that the old pyramid is the appropriate way to structure once again? The environment may fluctuate less wildly, but it is hardly predictable. It certainly isn't, nor will it ever be, the way it was before 1973. The halcyon days of noncompetitive, regulated, profit-guaranteed, stodgy banking are over. Banks and banking will never be the same.

But their structures are! Banks are losing ground to their nonbank competitors in terms of profitability and customer service. Large banks cannot compete with smaller banks in these two important areas. The reason is, they have not changed the way they structure themselves. They have not looked at the design of their work, the focus of their units, or the deployment of their management and other human resources.

Now is the time to tap that middle manager resource. All the literature in the quality field says that management, especially middle management, is a major barrier to quality improvement. Yet it is from these ranks that worker empowerment must come, and creative energy must be harnessed. Senior executives must be committed, workers must be brought actively into the process—but the real work is done in middle management by virtue of their relative freedom combined with their better perspective. Quality Value Engineering makes full use of this heretofore underutilized resource.

Of course, banks should not stop looking at ways to hone their management structure, to trim it where necessary, to make use of new norms regarding spans of control and new technology that may make certain manager functions unnecessary. Merely cutting middle manager levels and positions is not the answer. Rethinking those positions, redesigning work processes, and redefining the appropriate role of middle management is an answer, especially in conjunction with an organized and thoughtful program of resource reallocation. Only banks in danger of bankruptcy have the luxury of considering only the short-term advantages to cost-cutting; most banks must curb their reactive reduction programs, take the long view, and reconcile themselves to short-term pain for long-term gain.

A NEW WAY TO ORGANIZE

If the military model is no longer the appropriate paradigm, what is? The military itself provides an alternative.

In January 1991, the Persian Gulf War, although not over, was already a noticeably successful campaign. One of the salient features of this campaign was the use of coalition forces from a number of countries—the United States, Great Britain, Kuwait, Saudi Arabia, and Germany, among others. There were experts who predicted that the coalition forces could not succeed, or at least could not sustain success, because they were not united under a single military leader; in other words, the "unity of command" rule was expressly broken. And yet it succeeded admirably, in military terms, brilliantly even. If control and authority could not be used as coordinating mechanisms, what replaced them?

The *Los Angeles Times* analyzed it thus: "Unity of command was not an end in itself. The reason it is a principle of war is that it is the easiest way to ensure *unity of purpose*. But it is not the only way."[1] The coordinating device used by American and allied commanders was cooperation toward a single goal.

Political sensitivities, geographic distances, and functional differences may prevent the structural subordination of people and missions under a single command. Think of quality improvement teams which, although they may have a nominal leader to facilitate meetings and handle administrivia, don't really report to the team leader. Nevertheless, they are united by a sense of common purpose, and typically work more effectively than those who are united by organizational structure but are so fragmented or specialized that they do not share a common goal.

The military is making other changes. In May 1991, NATO restructured itself to establish "a smaller, more flexible military structure for Western Europe."[2] If the military is abandoning the military model, should banks cling to it?

Banks need to find modern analogs for the organizational rules that worked in the past but that are becoming increasingly ineffective now. The danger is that they may substitute semantic equivalencies rather than new ways of thinking and behaving. Keeping this caveat in mind, banks should follow some of the following new guidelines for organizational structure:

Old Language	New Language
Unity of command	Unity of purpose
Chain of command	Information linkages
Spans of control	Spheres of influence
Authority	Participation, cooperation, coordination
Manager	Leader
Manager	Coach
Subordinate	Team member

Note the two replacement terms for the word "manager." There are two distinct roles that managers are asked to assume, and while they are not mutually exclusive, most people are significantly more skilled in one area than the other. Leaders are the visionaries, the zealots, the missionaries; they bushwhack for the organization and tend to be intolerant of laggards. Coaches, on the other hand, are the champions and cheerleaders, the patient prodders of those who follow more slowly. Both are necessary; neither are managers as we think of them today, at least not of people.

CORPORATE TITLES

A somewhat peripheral yet relevant issue is that of corporate titles. It is the most visible trapping of bureaucracy and one that no American bank has tackled.[3] The problem with banking titles is twofold: those who don't have one waste a lot of time trying to get one; and hierarchy is literally built into them.

Banks have traditionally rewarded performance and longevity with titles rather than with money. For a long time, prestige has been a substitute for responsibility. Nearly everyone has a title. "Title inflation" is a catchphrase for the proliferation of titles. When there are too many vice presidents, banks create "first" vice presidents, then "senior" vice presidents, and so on. Although the titles become essentially meaningless, it is still better to be a have than a have-not in an organization that values them. The have-nots desire the prestige and the distinction that titles confer; they resent the haves, yet spend inordinate amounts of time trying to become one. Yet when there are hundreds and even thousands of vice presidents, what force does the title carry? Where is the achievement?

A more important problem is the hierarchy that is implied in these titles. It hampers flexibility and responsiveness to changing conditions. How can a first vice president report to an assistant vice president? It just isn't done. The organizational requirements change, and maybe what the assistant vice president is doing has become strategically more important than the first vice president's area of responsibility. Psychologically, the bank is stuck. It can't break the implicit hierarchy.

The major argument in defense of titles is that the customer demands to deal with a vice president. But is that really true? Has anyone asked customers recently? Most people deal with tellers, and they certainly don't carry vice president titles. And the majority of customers are savvy enough to understand the game that is played with titles; they don't take them seriously.

Corporate titles could be replaced with functional titles that better describe what the employees actually do and their level of experience in doing it. Suddenly the organization's structure, deployment of human resources, and working relationships can be viewed in a whole new light. Skilled employees can more easily be moved around in a strategic reorganization. Flexibility is automatically enhanced.

Team identity and collaboration might be improved by removing these artificial barriers, and instead of being one of hundreds of vice presidents, a manager can take pride in being the sole manager of a given area of expertise. Perhaps the uniqueness would encourage all the people in that group to make it the best it can be. And consider the increased potential for interfunctional teaming. Imagine, first of all, a meeting of the vice president of marketing, the senior vice president of retail banking, the assistant vice president of cost accounting, and the product manager to discuss the introduction of a new product. It is easy to guess who will do the most and the least talking. Contrast this with a meeting of representatives from marketing, retail banking, the new product, and cost accounting. This is a meeting of equals. As functional experts, each will be expected to contribute to and participate in the discussion and decision-making. No one can dominate by virtue of an irrelevant title.

Studies show that meaningful participation can result in increased productivity. As a communication barrier, titles reduce participation; it therefore follows that titles decrease potential productivity. Furthermore, titles are expensive, in terms of increases in base salary to higher standard benefits to the perquisites of executive titles, such as cars, car phones, executive services, and so on. Clearly, titles are a cost of quality—discussed in detail in Chapter 3—that can be eliminated for savings in hard and soft dollars.

Eliminating titles may be frightening for executives who rule on the strength of them, but it would be liberating for the

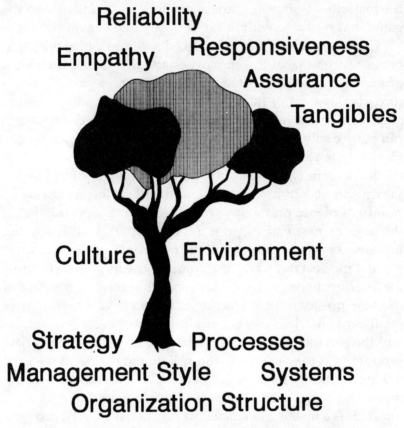

Reliability
Empathy Responsiveness
Assurance
Tangibles

Culture Environment

Strategy Processes
Management Style Systems
Organization Structure

Figure 1.3. Root Causes of Service Quality Gaps

rest. Banks cannot afford anything less than full participation from all employees. They will have to learn to shed their hierarchical ways and embrace the collaborative approach. A significant first step is to dismiss old and meaningless titles and focus on the contribution that each member of the organization can make.

THE ROOT CAUSE OF POOR QUALITY

The model shown in Figure 1.3 portrays the organization as a tree: The organization structure forms the roots; the environment is the trunk in which flows the lifeblood, the environment

ment is the trunk in which flows the lifeblood, the environment and culture, of the organization; and the culmination of growth are the branches. Organization structure may branch in many ways, but the five branches this book focuses on are the five dimensions of service quality: responsiveness, reliability, assurance, empathy, and tangibles.[4] As there is no one-to-one correspondence between a given root and a given branch, neither can one organization issue be solely responsible for one service quality gap. Rather, as the roots grow, so grows the tree—crooked, straight, strong, or weak.

Table 1.1 lists some of the organizational "red flags" that indicate a problem with structure and work design and traces them through the environment and on to the service quality areas. For instance, in-branch surveys show that customers are unhappy with what they perceive as low responsiveness on the part of the tellers. In other words, when they have a special request, transaction, or need, the tellers just don't seem to be able to handle it. They either put customers off with a canned answer or refer them to someone else. Tracing this problem through the environment, activities, and structure shows how root problems here can result in service quality issues. For example, interfunctional communication may be very low, so that tellers don't know how or where to get the information they need. Looking at employee activity reports confirms that employee and internal communication activities command relatively few resources in time and money. Structurally, the extra layers of management probably hamper and filter communication, slowing the tellers' response time further.

AN ORGANIZATIONAL SELF-ASSESSMENT

Tables 1.2 and 1.3 provide a list of red flags along with norms that have been developed over the years. The norms, however, must be taken with a lump of salt, because they are quite general and require massaging to match a given bank's conditions. Still, if any statistics are way off these norms, a bank probably has an area worth investigating.

Table 1.1 Organizing for Quality

Structure	Activities	Environment	Service Quality
Transaction info comes from several areas	Low training time and $	Training is on-the-job	Reliability—ability to perform the promise dependably and accurately
Physical and organizational distance between related departments	Proportionately small systems $	Systems/tools out of date	Responsiveness—willingness to help customers and to provide prompt service
Excess layers of management hamper communication	Fragmented job profiles	Pressure to get job done	Empathy—caring, individualized attention provided to customers
Hierarchical: no teams	Fragmented processes and low horizontal or vertical integration	Interfunctional communication very low—don't know where to get information to do job	Assurance—knowledge and courtesy of employees and their ability to convey trust and confidence
Small spans—lots of specialized groups	Sales activities high, "existing business" low	Rewards for productivity	Tangibles—physical attributes such as facilities, appearance
Strict chain of command	"Complaints" cited more than "inquiries"	Employees last to know	
Strict functional segmentation and small spans	Duplication of activities	Supervisors care only about getting job done	
Duplicated functions—centralized and decentralized	Lots of verification activities	Sell first, service second	
High ratio of managers to workers and staff to line	Low managing time	Not free to make decisions	
	High focus on prime activities, but few customer activities	Too much fire-fighting	
		Unable to speak freely or to suggest improvements	
		Low morale—dissatisfaction with salary	

16

Table 1.2 Structural Analysis Checklist and Benchmarks

Red Flag	Structural Norms	Comments
Small spans	Dependent—rarely less than 6	Ideally, "stretch" spans should be assigned before starting the analysis. Small spans are justified by different shifts and locations, small volumes of work, and specialization. Otherwise, extra manager positions may be indicated.
Large spans	Rarely greater than 20	Cause problems with manager burnout, insufficient direction and supervision of employees, ineffective management of function.
One-over-one and one-over-two reporting	Spans of between 6 and 20	Almost always indicates too many managers; often a factor of an inadequate compensation policy.
Duplicate functional units	One unit per function	Verify that activities performed, not just the names, are the same. Evaluate the possibility of consolidating the units. Hard or soft dollar savings may be realized by eliminating a manager position.
Odd functional groupings	Consistent, supplementary, or complementary missions within functions	Determine the reasons for and the results of the unusual grouping. May indicate empire-building or service quality problems that need to be addressed separately. Probably a dysfunctional arrangement to some extent, detracting from primary mission(s) of area.
Ratio of managers to workers	Overall organization: 1:8 Staff areas: 1:10 Clerical units: 1:15 Professional: 1:12	Ideal ratios depend on several factors: nature of work (routine/nonroutine) performed; homogeneity of work; training and education level of workers; amount of direct supervision required; level of manager; and others. Calculate by dividing number of workers by number of managers.
Cents to manage	Overall organization: $0.40 Staff areas: $0.35 Clerical units: $0.20 Professional: $0.45	Cents to manage is inversely rated to the manager/worker ratio; calculate by dividing manager salaries by worker salaries.

Table 1.3 Work Distribution Analysis Checklist

Red Flag	Work Distribution Norms	Comments
Excess or insufficient individual managing time	Supervisor: 25–30% Middle manager: 35–50% Senior manager: 50–60%	Generally, first- and second-level managers are somewhat "hands on" managers, becoming more "professional managers" farther up in the organization.
High proportion of support time and of high or low managing time overall	Prime: At least 65% Support: Less than 20% Managing: Not more than 15%	High support time may indicate suboptimal productivity; high managing time may indicate too much bureaucracy; low managing time may indicate an overall lack of direction.
Many activities reported by an individual	8–10 activities per person	Too many activities may indicate a lack of job focus, a "workaholic" employee, or a poor understanding of job requirements. Job fragmentation results in a lot of stop-and-start, wasted time in preparation and processing.
Activities duplicated in different areas	Mission-related activities performed primarily in unit with that mission	Some generic, especially support, activities (e.g., clerical work) will be performed throughout the organization. A lack of focus, coordination, and synergy may result from prime activities being performed in several places. Question to ask: Are the right people doing the right activities, in the right places, for the right amount of time?
High amounts of paperwork-related work	Clerical and related work: less than 10% overall	Excess paperwork wastes resources and indicates need for analysis of processes and products.

The organizational assessment worksheet at the end of this chapter will enable a bank to assess the state of its organization structure. The worksheet can be used for the bank overall or for any of its components. Some of the information can't be gauged precisely without significant data collection; it can be guesstimated, however, by interviewing representative samples of various functional areas. Most of the information will be available from a current organization chart and the human resources information system or payroll system.

The worksheet can't gauge the opportunities for collaborative work by employees, the general level of morale, or the level of internal and external customer service quality in the organization. What it will do is show a bank where there may be barriers in the form of poor structure as measured by simple arithmetic techniques and applied against industry norms. If a bank's organization is flat, spans and ratios high, cents to manage (an overhead measure) low, and activities properly placed, it is in better shape than most to move ahead with a quality improvement program (although if the numbers are this good, the bank probably already has). If a bank falls short in one or more areas, it will know where to begin an investigation to ferret out the structural causes of poor quality that affect the ability to serve customers.

What follows in *Quality Value Banking* is predicated on improving structure, management style, and the systems and processes that contribute to the service quality gaps banks have. The book teaches the methodology of Quality Value Engineering for making improvements, narrowing the gaps, and increasing the productivity and financial performance of the bank.

ORGANIZATIONAL ASSESSMENT WORKSHEET

Cents to manage (managers' salaries divided by
    workers' salaries) $0._____

Ratio of managers to workers (number of workers
    divided by number of managers)   1: _____

Layers of management (between chief executive and
    workers)   _____

Average span of control (average number of direct reports)   _____

Instances of one-over-one or one-over-two reporting
    relationships   _____

Number of different activities performed by employees   _____

Number of support activities performed by employees   _____

Amount of time spent managing by managers and
    supervisors   _____

Functions and activities performed in more than one place:

Activity/Function	*Where Performed*
_____	_____
	_____
	_____

Analysis of Common Support Activities
Number of Reports Produced _____ Frequency _____
No. of Copies Distributed   _____
Hours Spent in Meetings Weekly (all participants × hours)   _____
Number of Complaints Received (daily, weekly, monthly
    as appropriate)   _____

Handled By	Department	Right Person?	How Handled?
_____	_____	_____	_____

    What are the primary reasons for the complaints?

Number of People Involved in "Special Projects"   _____

    Nature of the special projects:

    Duration and benefit of the projects:

NOTES

1. Harry G. Summers, Jr., "Some Notions of Naysayers Bite the Dust," *Los Angeles Times*, January 21, 1991, p. A9; emphasis added.

2. Melissa Healy, "NATO Votes to Restructure Its Military Forces," *Los Angeles Times*, May 29, 1991, p. A1.

3. Royal Trust Bank of Ontario, Canada, has replaced its corporate titles with "partner" titles, used by the president on down. A year and a half after the completion of the program, the bank professes to be "delighted" with the results, which include a distinct alteration of the way employees think about and relate to each other at all levels.

4. The five dimensions of service quality are taken from Len Berry's work with David R. Bennett and Carter W. Brown in *Service Quality: A Profit Strategy for Financial Institutions* (Homewood, Ill.: Dow Jones-Irwin, 1989); and with Valarie A. Zeithaml and A. Parasuraman in *Delivering Quality Service: Balancing Customer Perceptions and Expectations*. (New York: Free Press, 1990).

Chapter 2

The Banker's World Has Changed

The year was 1980. The trading room at Union Commerce Bank,[1] the lead bank in a $1.2 billion bank holding company in Cleveland, Ohio, was in a state of confusion. Cigarette smoke hung three or four feet from the ceiling; its density increased by the minute. Coffee sat cold and stale in styrofoam cups. It was 4:00 P.M. Gerry Donovan, vice president of the funds management group and head trader, had just called.

"Tom, I can't get enough money. Rates have skyrocketed. Fed Funds are selling at 21 percent and nobody's willing to sell. Bob and Susan are talking to the West Coast banks right now, but we're not going to make it. It's 4:00 P.M., and I'm $30 million short."

Screens of green numbers blinked. Phones rang and were answered. The traders tried to buy money anywhere they could, even at 21 percent.

"We're going to have to go to The Window," Gerry said over the din in the trading room.

"We can't. We've never done that. We can't let the Fed know we're in trouble."

"It's either let them know, or we're out of business. We can't raise the money. Call them."

"We've got to tell Tim. We're not going to the Fed with him not knowing."

"I don't care who you have to call. We don't have much time. Call the Fed."

Tim Treadway, the CEO, was advised, the call was made, and the Federal Reserve Bank came to the rescue.

CHANGES IN THE INDUSTRY

The scene described above was not uncommon during the early 1980s. Rates that were normally stable were all over the place. New products were being offered. Banks were charging for services that had previously been free. Competitors were crawling out of the woodwork—foreign banks, nonbank banks, Sears, for heaven's sake! Everything was different.

Since that day, there have been events in the financial services industry that no one could have conceived of in 1980. Think of the deregulation of the liability side of the balance sheet with DIDMCA and Garn–St. Germain and the weakening of the Glass–Steagall Act. There were the hostile takeovers of Union Commerce by Huntington Bancshares and Irving Trust by Bank of New York. Penn Square failed and threatened to take Continental Illinois and Seafirst with it. Bank of New England proved that no bank is too big to fail, though it was eventually rescued by the FDIC. There were mergers of huge banks such as NCNB and C&S/Sovran as they formed NationsBank. NOW accounts and money market accounts, deposits that earlier bankers never knew, became staples of the balance sheet. Funds were transmitted at the speed of light between banks all over the world. Tellers knew account balances instantaneously, and probably had more accurate figures about them than most of us did. ATMs provided customers with the ability to conduct a myriad of transactions without ever having to see a teller.

Banks crossed state lines, something that the McFadden Act of 1927 said they could not do. The world had become very different for the banks, yet many had failed to determine a successful direction and strategy. The industry was in trouble, primarily because many of the nation's bankers still did not see that they had to conduct the affairs of their institutions differently than in the past when regulation told them what to do and how to do it. Most of them had a great deal of trouble dealing with the disorder in the financial services industry which for years had been so calm.

In the midst of all of this confusion, several banks managed to weather the storm of change and showed increasing profits. That could not be said for all of them, however. Losses became commonplace as many banks were caught with concentrations of assets in deals that went bad. They were incurred by such stalwart institutions as Ameritrust, Fleet/Norstar, Chase Manhattan, MNC Financial, Bank of Boston, and Shawmut National. Further, many banks, Citicorp, PNC Financial, First Chicago, C&S, Barnett Banks, Security Pacific, NCNB, and Mellon among them, reported earnings lower than in previous years. Prior to the 1980s, very few banks posted losses or lower quarter-to-quarter earnings, but in that decade, it was a most common occurrence. Obviously, the world had changed.

To make matters even worse, the failure rate continued to be high. Almost 1,200 commercial and savings banks failed in the 1980s alone. The projection was that more would fail in the 1990s. The big news, of course, was the FDIC's seizure of Bank of New England early in January 1991, which went bankrupt because its losses from real estate loans exceeded its equity

Table 2.1 Consolidation in the Banking Industry

	1980	1990
New charters	205	165
Consolidation, absorbed, and merged	132	390
Failures	10	159*
Number of banks	14,435	12,338
Number of branches	38,736**	51,225
Number of multibank holding companies	284	831
Number of banks owned by MBHCs	2,269	3,780

Source: ABA Banking Journal (August 1991):31.

*Failures peaked in 1988 with 221.

**Includes ATMs in 1980.

capital. Industry experts predicted that there would be a continued consolidation of the nation's 12,000 banks with less than half of them surviving. Recent predictions have since lowered the amount of shrinkage from 50 to 20 percent or less, but a net loss of as many as 2,400 banks is no small thing. Table 2.1 shows the consolidation that has already occurred in the industry between 1980 and 1990.

NEW COMPETITION EMERGED

In what used to be a very balanced situation, there was sudden instability. On the one hand were banks with high earnings; on the other, a steady failure rate, losses, and, to complicate matters, increasing domestic and foreign competition. Market share vis-à-vis nonbank competition was decreasing, as Figure 2.1 shows. The percentage of total assets held by commercial banks was 26.6 percent in 1990, down from 34.2 percent in 1960.[2] Figure 2.2 demonstrates that in 1960 the banks held 70

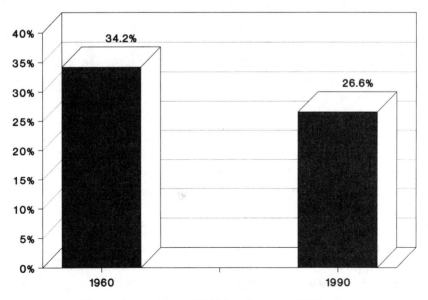

Figure 2.1. Assets Held by Commercial Banks

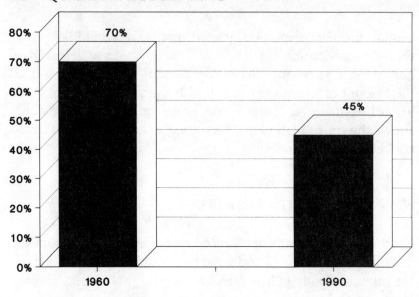

Figure 2.2. Commercial and Industrial Loans of Commercial Banks

percent of the country's commercial and industrial loans, decreasing to 45 percent in 1990.[3] Corporate borrowers who used to go to the bank could now go to a variety of other sources for financing, such as General Motors Acceptance Corporation or General Electric Capital Corporation, and could venture into the commercial paper and bond markets as well.

Individual consumers also had more choices. In 1986, the share of receivables held by credit card companies other than banks was $5.0 billion as Figure 2.3 shows. At the end of 1990, that had jumped to $30.1 billion. The credit card market used to be the sole proprietorship of the banks, beginning at Flatbush National Bank in New York City in 1946. Now, with American Express, Discover, AT&T, MBNA, and others delivering better service at often lower rates, the consumer had many more choices.

There were also new alternative deposit opportunities. Consumers had money market funds, mutual funds, tax-exempt bonds, the stock market, and other instruments from which to choose in addition to the traditional accounts pro-

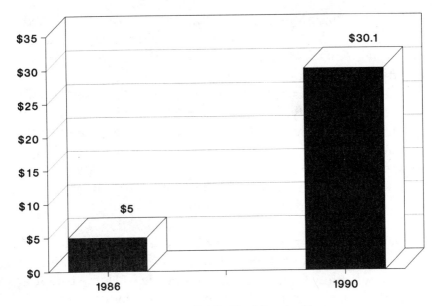

Figure 2.3. Credit Card Receivables

vided by the commercial banks. Many savers began to place their deposits where the interest rate was highest and the potential for growth was present, and acted as though they did not care about having deposit insurance anymore.

Competition from overseas continued to increase as well. Foreign banks accounted for 30 percent of all commercial and industrial loans in the United States as the 1980s came to a close.[4]

FUNDAMENTAL QUESTIONS AROSE

No one, in 1980, would have forecasted all of this or that there would be even more changes that would alter completely the ways the banks would operate. In the early 1990s, serious questions about the entire banking industry were being asked. Were there going to be only ten meganational banks like Bank of America and Citicorp? Were the established money center banks like Chase Manhattan really obsolete? Did the United States need 12,000 commercial banks? Would the huge regional banks like NBD and First Wachovia be able to serve the demands of their customers?

Would the banks be able to continue to reduce their physical size and capacity? The merger of Manufacturer's Hanover and Chemical on the East Coast and Security Pacific and Bank of America on the West Coast promised to achieve significant economies of scale, but would they get them? Mergers of smaller banks would continue to take place as well, as capital became scarcer and expenses continued to grow faster than income.

Where would banking go technologically? PCs were in their infancy in 1980, but their capabilities were expanding almost every day both within the bank and outside it. Home banking became a reality. Electronic delivery systems moved funds all over the world at the punch of a button, making gathering deposits considerably faster and easier.

Would the banks be able to branch across the nation? Regulation had precluded interstate banking, except in cases of reciprocity and potential failure, but the new competition wasn't subject to it. GMAC, American Express, and Sears were the first "national banks," and entered the markets that had been exclusively those of the banks. Some banks, however, such as First Interstate, BancOne, First of America, and Key-Bank, were starting to gain a national presence.

Would bankers continue to focus on the short term? Would they continue to concentrate on next quarter's earnings and not worry about the effect of their decisions on the longer term? Would bankers start thinking strategically about satisfying the customer's future financial services demands, not about increasing the fee for an NSF check $2 next quarter?

Questions have been asked over and over again. "What happened?" "How did we get into this mess?" "How can we get out of it?" "Do the banks have time?" This book is dedicated to answering the first three questions; the answer to the fourth is uncertain.

THE BASICS OF BANKING

Any successful banker will relate the three fundamentals upon which that success has been based. First, the bank must have a stable and sound core deposit base. Second, it must have sound lending practices. Third, it must diversify, distributing its loans into a variety of industries and geographic locations in order to spread its risk.

Banking is not a complex process. In fact, banking used to be easy. Banks take in deposits from customers, paying an acceptable rate of interest for them, and then lend these deposited amounts to borrowers for houses, automobiles, schooling, business expansion, and a whole variety of other purposes. Prior to 1975, the rate charged the borrower would be 3 or 4 percent more than was being paid to the depositor so the bank would have sufficient income to pay its people, have a facility in which to transact business, and return a small dividend to its shareholders. When core deposits remained fairly stable and the overall rate of interest paid did not vary much, the bank was assured of lending profitably to its customers.

The loan was the key. If the borrower was creditworthy and made the required interest and principal repayments, the bank was fine. When customers were unable to make those payments, the bank suffered. Knowing the customer and having good collateral were essential.

The last basic is diversification. To diversify is to distribute the loan portfolio evenly across industries so that if there is a problem in one area of the economy, the bank only has a portion of its risk there. Each time there has been a problem in the industry, it has been caused by a concentration of loans in a narrowly defined market. Since the 1970s, there have been several times when the industry as a whole, as well as individual banks, have failed to keep a diversified portfolio: REITs (real estate investment trusts) in the 1970s; junk bonds, loans to Latin American countries, and HLTs (highly leveraged transactions) in the 1980s; and real estate in the 1990s.

Diversification also means spreading into different geographic areas. The idea is to enter emerging markets with services that meet the demands of customers to offset any declines in the ones the bank already serves. As populations moved out of cities into suburbs, for example, and from the north to the south, banks that did not diversify geographically saw their markets decline and eventually disappear. This notion was one of the key factors in the drive for interstate banking.

For a bank to stay out of financial trouble, Dave Hanick, then chief financial officer of National City Bank, gave some sound advice: "Look, we're not greedy. We take our share of the pie and are happy with it, and we're OK. We have an international portfolio, and it's had its share of problems. We lost $75 million over a period of 5 years, but you never saw an earnings blip. We're conservative. It's diversification. Credit can put you out of business fast, and when it starts, there's nothing you can do about it."[5]

The lesson to be learned from these experiences is know the customers, have a stable deposit base, make sound loans, and diversify.

WHAT HAPPENED?

The answer to this question is embedded in the history of banking during the twentieth century. This book will not chronicle all of the events in American banking, nor will it contain all of the details in the scenes that are described. Rather it will demonstrate the circumstances that led the financial services industry to its current condition and offer some suggestions as to what can be done to prevent it from happening again.

The key events that need to be understood are:

- The stock market crash of October 1929
- Enactment of the Glass–Steagall Act, 1933
- Organization of the Federal Deposit Insurance Corporation, 1935
- Opening of new financial markets

- Introduction of the money market account
- The shift in monetary policy in 1979

Each of these events changed the banker's world completely and in its own way.

The Stock Market Crash

On October 29, 1929, the stock market crashed, taking thousands of investors with it. The banks were also in trouble since many of them had made loans to help finance the incredible run-up of the market in the previous months. When borrowers pledged stock as collateral for loans, and their value decreased, banks were faced with assets on their books that would never be repaid. These bad loans had to be charged-off, which weakened the banks' capital position, threatened depositors, and forced many of them to close.

The stock market crash initiated the Great Depression, which lasted well into the 1930s. By July 1932, the market had reached its lowest point—worth one-tenth of what it had been in September 1929.[6] Industrial production fell, there was no demand for loans, and nobody had any money to deposit. Unemployment increased to 25 percent of the workforce. Banks were closing daily, with 1,350 shutting their doors in 1930; 2,293 in 1931; and 1,453 in 1932.[7]

The politicians and the American people blamed the banks for the crash and subsequent Depression. It was an easy way out. As early as January 1933, the Senate started to investigate Wall Street to determine what had happened. With the vision of unending unemployment lines, steadily falling prices, lost savings, and dismal personal futures firmly in mind, the outcome of these inquiries would change the way in which bankers would be viewed for generations.

Banks were supposed to be safe havens for hard-earned savings and bankers were supposed to be trustworthy. In the period before the crash, however, there had been greed, irresponsibility, and violation of public trust, especially when banks tried to cover themselves by acquiring assets of greater risk, knowing that if they defaulted, they could fail and take depositors down as well.

In 1933, nobody realized, however, that the events leading to the crash of October 1929, and those that followed, would change the ways Americans would do business forever. It would have been impossible, then, to see how the federal government would change the role of the banks, restricting them from certain, specific activities, which would lead others to fill the void.

The politicians in Washington in the early 1930s perceived that the combination of commercial and investment banking was the cause of the problem, and the movement to separate the two functions began. Whether it was the fact that the banks were allowed to do both or whether it was the abuse of the ability to do them is a matter of conjecture, but the perception that it was the cause was sufficient to inspire political action.

Further, as more and more of the insider dealings of the banks became known, public as well as political feelings hardened against them. The bankers had made loans to each other, often at preferential rates. They sat on each other's boards of directors, obviously a conflict of interest. They were bankers to the biggest companies in America and held influence in their boardrooms as well. It is reported, for example, that partners in the J. P. Morgan Company held "126 directorships in 89 corporations with $20 billion in assets."[8]

In short, the power of the banks before the crash was enormous. But that was about to change. The mood of the country was angry, because their trust in the banks had been violated. They would never let that happen again. "For reasons that have never been entirely clear, there has always existed within the American public a deeply ingrained fear of banking power. Power, inevitably, was viewed as a concomitant of size, and size in turn was likely to be the result of permitting relatively few institutions to engage in banking."[9]

The Glass–Steagall Act of 1933
and the Banking Act of 1935

Senator Carter Glass of Virginia and Alabama Representative Henry Steagall authored congressional legislation that would change the ways banks would be able to do business for the next 50 years.

The Glass–Steagall Act prohibited banks from engaging in both the investment and commercial banking functions; limited interstate banking by leaving that decision to the states (which didn't want it); and contained an innovation—federal deposit insurance—which changed the behavior of the banker and the consumer. The backlash from the stock market crash and subsequent Great Depression was so strong that the American people told their legislators, in essence, "Don't let that ever happen to us again." If they couldn't trust the banks, but had no other place to put their hard-earned savings, they wanted to be sure that they would never suffer loss again, hence the insurance. In reality, Glass–Steagall did something very different.

Deposit insurance was actually a government subsidy that made bankers less accountable. Once they realized that if their loans defaulted and had to be charged-off to capital with the potential of insolvency, but that the depositor would be made whole by the FDIC, the incentive for making absolutely sure about a customer and the requested loan was diminished. The banker did not have to be as careful, which was what the law was trying to ensure. The banks could acquire riskier assets this way, hoping for a higher return to satisfy those short-term earnings projections. This provision became a safety net to the banker as well as to the depositor, with the rest of the country paying for it.

Glass–Steagall also established Regulation Q, which set ceilings on savings interest rates. The purpose of Reg Q was to abolish bidding wars for deposits, effectively eliminating competition for them. For the first time, the government had put cost controls on the banks; they would not disappear for almost 50 years. Regulation Q was aimed at stabilizing the American banking system and ensured that banks would no longer be allowed to pay depositors whatever they wanted. This would keep the cost of funds down. Reg Q eliminated the need to acquire risky assets, counterbalancing the effect of the new deposit insurance to encourage it. The ceilings on interest rates paid to depositors were certainly acceptable to the small saver whose memory of the Depression was still rather fresh, and who therefore was willing to trade income for security.

With all of this legislation, banking became easy. Banks had defined markets in which they could compete, since the states would not let them venture into new ones. The government dictated what they could pay their suppliers (i.e., depositors), and the prime rate became their published price. The bankers could not influence either rate very much. Because those competitive forces were held in check, the industry as a whole lost its vitality and creativity.

Two years later, Congress passed the Banking Act of 1935 and created the Federal Deposit Insurance Corporation as an agency of the U.S. government. In doing so, it made the concept of deposit insurance permanent. The American people liked the idea of knowing that their money was insured if the bank became insolvent. As time passed, the bankers, too, were at ease with the concept of deposit insurance, and they knew that if the institution failed because of the inability of their customers to service their debt, depositors would be protected.

The 1935 act also authorized the FDIC to take action to keep banks that were in trouble from failing, something that has been under scrutiny in the "Too Big to Fail" argument. It was to play a major role in regulating the banks and in keeping them from failure. If it had not done so, banks that defaulted might have triggered further collapses, creating the domino effect experienced in the crash throughout the American financial system after the 1929 crash. The 1935 act also gave the FDIC regulatory authority over all banks that were not supervised by either the Federal Reserve or the Comptroller of the Currency, most notably state-chartered banks that had chosen not to join the Federal Reserve System.

It was at this point that the regulatory powers of the federal government were at an all time high, completing the reaction to the speculation of the 1920s and the Depression of the early 1930s. In a period of ten years the financial mood in the United States had changed completely from the "go-go" 1920s when the banks were fueling the tremendous growth, to 1935 when the banks were being told what they could do, the price they could charge, and the markets in which they could compete; were subject to rigorous examinations; and were funding the FDIC insurance pool.

From a position of great wealth and political and economic power, the banks were now under the direct control of the federal government. As the country endured the Great Depression:

- banks had to choose whether to be commercial or investment
- Regulation Q had set the ceiling on the payment of interest rates
- most of the people were blaming the banks for it
- the FDIC was in place, insuring individual deposits and carefully watching troubled banks
- the Federal Reserve had assumed greater power and was now centrally located in Washington, D.C.

The Glass–Steagall Act and the Banking Act of 1935 completely restrained the banks. They were being punished for the crash of October 1929 and the Great Depression. The lawmakers wanted to make certain that all the banks did was take deposits and make prudent loans. And that's what banks did. For the next 50 years, there was little freedom in banking. With Reg Q still in place and the prime rate not fluctuating very much, banking was, indeed, easy.

The New Banking Game

After World War II, in the unparalleled economic growth that is the one benefit of war, soldiers returned from the Pacific and European theaters to settle back into their lives. They wanted to purchase homes and went to the local savings and loan, not the bank, to obtain financing. The S&Ls were not subject to Glass–Steagall or the Banking Act of 1935 so they were able to pay their customers higher rates of interest for deposits than the banks were allowed to pay. They were making loans for houses day and night and had the banks at a rate disadvantage.

Even so, everything worked well until the mid-1960s, when some of the S&Ls decided to pay a significant premium for deposits and a rate war ensued. In 1967, therefore, Congress put the S&Ls under the restraints of Regulation Q, but allowed them to pay 0.5 percent more for deposits than the banks to encourage consumer savings and their redeployment into housing. This put some stability into the financial markets, but the banks were still at a competitive disadvantage, and not only from the S&Ls.

The federal government also got into the act. While the banks were limited to the rates they could pay depositors for their funds, the government was not. It set rates on its securities higher than the banks could pay, high enough to attract investors and, as with FDIC insurance, provided security with the "full faith and credit" of the U.S. government behind them.

In response, First National City Bank of New York (now Citicorp), began offering a new savings instrument called a certificate of deposit (CD) in 1961. It had a fixed term, carried a higher interest rate than passbook savings, and allowed the bank to attract deposits from sources that would have otherwise invested them in government securities. This was the first challenge to Regulation Q. Other banks followed, and by the end of 1961, CDs totaling $1 billion were sitting on the balance sheets of the nation's banks.

There was a subtle change relative to the introduction of

CDs, however. The bank's cost of funds increased. If it had to pay a higher rate to get the deposit, its average cost of funds went up. When that happened, the margin started to narrow, and all things being equal, earnings decreased. To offset that increased cost of funds, the bank would have to obtain higher rates on its loans, which meant assuming more risk. It would have to start financing projects that might not have been acceptable to its loan committee in prior times. That additional risk, whether in the form of an LDC, a junk bond, or a piece of real estate, was the subtlety. To cover the increasing cost of funds, if a bank wanted to keep the margin spread near the same percentage, it had to take on more risk.

CDs allowed banks to compete for deposits with the S&Ls, as well as the federal government, but by paying the higher rates, their interest margin was narrowing and Regulation Q and Glass–Steagall were being tested. Near the end of the 1980s, there was $183 billion of CDs in the American banks, compared to $1 billion 27 years before.

The Challenge to the Regulations Continued

The advent of the Eurodollar market was the second chip at Glass–Steagall. The banks could take their deposits and place them overseas where rates were not regulated and fluctuated at market values. They could buy money whenever and wherever they pleased instead of trying to entice their current customers to increase their deposits or to find new ones, but that also cost them more.

Eurodollar markets gave the bankers of the 1960s considerably more freedom, at the expense of the margin; they also offered bankers an opportunity to invest in the riskier international arenas where they had never been before. Many of them were not qualified to be there and saw their loans in these foreign countries go bad.

Not only was the liability side beginning to open up in the 1960s, but another event occurred that affected the loan side: the advent of commercial paper, an instrument developed to allow the nation's corporations to access the money markets for financing without having to go to the banks. Typically, these corporations had high credit ratings, which meant that risk of default was low, causing commercial paper to be an attractive investment alternative. For the banks, that meant that interest income decreased, which narrowed the margin even more. Not only were they paying more for their money now, in terms of CDs and Eurodollars, but they were also earning less since their commercial customers were going into the markets themselves.

There were, however, some companies that couldn't do so, and in order to provide them with an adequate source of funding, the Federal Reserve suspended Regulation Q on all CDs over $100,000 in 1973. That allowed the banks to compete freely in the money markets to satisfy the cash requirements of their corporate customers.

However, with the ceiling off—and it would be difficult to reimpose it—the cost of funds rose again; and if the funds could not be deployed at a sufficient spread, the margin was narrowing even more. Regulation Q had suffered its third attack.

Merrill Lynch Introduces the CMA

The blow that signaled the death of Regulation Q came in 1975, when Merrill Lynch introduced its cash management account (CMA). For the first time in 40 years, individual depositors had the option of placing funds with a financial institution that was offering deposits, investment management, and stock brokerage services from the same location.

The CMA paid a higher rate of interest than the banks could pay under Reg Q, allowed a certain number of checks to be written, and did not require a minimum balance (which many kinds of bank services did). There was no deposit insurance, but the reputations of the firms selling these services (in addition to Merrill-Lynch, Salomon Brothers, E. F. Hutton, Goldman Sachs, and Shearson offered these accounts) and the companies in which they invested were first-rate. There was little risk, which was the reason that over $230 billion left the banks for the brokerage houses between their introduction and late 1982.

Reg Q did not allow banks to retaliate. It had been in place for 45 years. That's about five generations of bankers. They had built infrastructures, branch delivery systems, automated computer systems, huge organizational hierarchies, and bureaucratic ways of doing business, thinking that the world would never change. They never thought that they would have to compete with anybody but First National from across the street.

Banks could not compete on cost and price since the Fed told them what interest rates would be, and price was not an issue because of the dependence on the prime rate. But, now, with rates fluctuating at market values and this huge disintermediation to the brokerages, banks knew that they had to fight back.

The World Turned Upside Down

It was going to get worse. On October 6, 1979, Paul Volcker, the chairman of the Federal Reserve, declared war on inflation and tight money was going to be the weapon. The money supply would remain stable and interest rates would be variable. This shift in policy caused the short-term rates to reach heretofore unheard of levels, much like the scenario painted at the beginning of this chapter. Rates were so high that many institutions were faced with fixed rate assets on their books earning less than the rates being paid to fund them. Further, with rates at these levels, bankers had to quit making deals because the cost of funds was higher than the rates they could earn. The savings and loan industry went into a tailspin, and the country slid into a recession. "The impact of stagflation and high interest rates in the early 1970s had dire consequences for banking during the late 1980s. The financial and economic machinations that took place at the macro (Federal) level made sound financial judgements at the micro (bank) level very difficult."[10]

Deposits were racing to the money market funds; loans were yielding 8 to 18 percent; the cost of funds was anywhere from 10 to 21 percent; expenses continued to increase; fees were just starting to be charged and did not provide much relief; and charges to the loan loss provision began to increase.

The stability bankers had known for 50 years was gone as they watched their balance sheets and income statements behave very differently than ever before. They knew that regulation was restricting them from competing, and tried to circumvent that problem by entering the newer financial markets. Most of them realized that the industry that they had once known would never return.

Their response was to put political pressure on Congress to change the laws. They realized their disadvantage, understanding that they were facing a new group of financial products that were not subject to the same regulations as theirs were. Something had to be done to Reg Q or their deposits would continue to disappear.

DIDMCA AND THE GARN–ST. GERMAIN ACT

Because the banks were caught in this competitive vise, Congress simply had no choice but to eliminate many of the regulations, not the least of which was Reg Q, and subsequently passed the Depository Institutions Deregulation and Monetary Control Act (DIDMCA) of 1980. The legislators finally comprehended that if the banks were not allowed to offer competitive financial services, many of them would not survive.

DIDMCA had two major provisions. First, it called for a six-year elimination of the ceilings on interest rates as required by Regulation Q. This would enable banks to pay market rates that would give them a better chance of keeping their customers' deposits. Second, it permitted interest to be paid on checking accounts. Banking customers would switch their funds from the traditional noninterest-bearing accounts to these that would pay for them, but at least the bank did not lose the deposit, even if its cost of funds increased again.

In essence, DIDMCA restored banks to where they had been 45 years before, at least on the deposit side of the ledger. Investment banking and commercial banking were still separated, but Reg Q, which restricted competition for funds, was to be a thing of the past.

However, the financial dilemma continued. Being able to have rates similar to those of the money market funds and paying interest on demand deposits allowed banks to compete equally in the financial markets, even if it took six years to achieve, but it did not relieve the downward pressure on the net interest margin. The days of "free" money, and the advantage it provided, were gone.

Two years later, on December 14, 1982, the Garn–St. Germain Act allowed the banks to replicate the Merrill Lynch CMA, enabling them finally to compete directly with the money market funds. For seven years they had watched as these funds had drained their deposits, but with Garn–St. Germain, they could try to get them back.

Slowly but surely, the regulations of the 1930s were being challenged and eliminated as the banks continued to fight for the ability to compete. They had watched as the new competition had invaded their markets and had no way to respond. Finally, they had been able to prevail in Congress. The economics, though, had not changed. Even with the new legislation, margins continued to suffer due to the higher cost of funds, causing the banks to try to find ways to compensate for that increase. They saw their fiscal condition deteriorating and were caught with a different financial structure.

In order to obtain higher returns, they began to make loans in areas where there was more exposure and risk, but where rates were sufficient to cover their increasing costs. "'It's the herd mentality. Banking, as a regulated industry, has it worse than anyone.' explains David Pringle, an analyst at Furman Selz Inc. in New York. 'Bankers admit it. For them, the right thing to do is always what everyone else is doing.' In the 1970s, it was lending to developing countries; in the mid-80s, it was financing highly leveraged transactions; in the late 1980s, it was real estate."[11] In the words of Doug Bannerman, senior vice president of National City Corporation, "We took our eye off the ball!" In many instances, banks forgot the three basics of banking—sound loans, stable core deposits, and diversification—while they were breaking out of their bureaucratic molds to venture into new territories.

Banks deployed their deposits into oil and gas, Latin America, junk bonds and other highly leveraged transactions (HLTs), and real estate, hoping for that big return that turned out not to be there. Many of them rolled the dice and came up short, which had a negative impact on shareholders, markets, customers, and employees.

Glass–Steagall should have been changed as soon as Merrill-Lynch brought out the CMA and the banks saw the new competition advancing into their markets. The success of banks depended on asset quality and diversification, but they also had to have a stable core deposit base. When that deposit base was under attack and $230 billion left the banks for the brokerage houses, everyone knew that the rules of the game had changed and that the banks were at a severe disadvantage. The regulations of the 1930s had not let them meet a changing world.

Furthermore, the correlation that had always held between a bank's deposits and its net operating income had significantly weakened, indicating that the ability to profitably borrow and lend money had likewise eroded.[12] Figure 2.4 shows that the correlation between deposits and earnings, that is, the bank's ability to make money, had been substantially damaged by the late 1980s. Although the numbers shown are for a particular bank, the Bank of North Dakota (BND), there are reasons to believe that the situation was even worse for most commercial banks, due to the special structure of BND.[13] The correlation between deposits and earnings (net operating income) between 1919 and 1969 is a strong .9, meaning that as deposits grew, earnings could be expected to grow at about the same rate. The correlation deteriorates to .62 in the period 1969 to 1985, and actually reverses itself in the years 1986 to 1988.

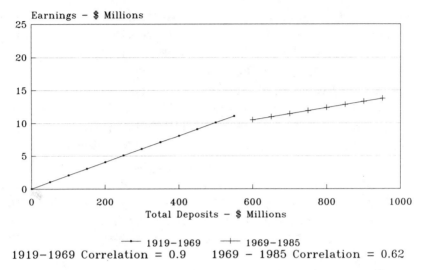

Figure 2.4. Correlation Between Deposits and Profit, 1919–1969 and 1969–1985

WHAT COULD THEY DO?

Hundreds of banks sacrificed long-term sustainable growth for short-term profits as they tried to keep their returns high for the investment community. Needing capital badly, they found themselves in direct competition with industrial and consumer companies for the investment dollar and had to show sufficient returns to warrant it.

Banks tried to increase their returns by investing in high-risk loans that they hoped would contribute to their capital structures. Many suffered huge losses instead. In response, the regulators raised the capital-to-asset ratio so that the banks had to keep at least 6 percent of their total assets in their capital accounts. At a time when their capital was being eroded by poor asset quality and less than average earnings, they were being told to increase it.

So the banks tried a new tactic, one that was even endorsed by the regulators themselves: to cut, or eliminate, the dividend being paid to shareholders who had invested in their common stock. Such a move was unprecedented in the industry. The situation in the 1980s was so drastic, with the survival of many of the country's largest banks at stake, that suspending the dividend was judged to be a necessity.

Banks also began to levy service charges and fees. Prior to the late 1970s, most bank services were free. The balances customers left in their accounts were invested in sound loans that returned enough to cover all of the bank's expenses. There were no monthly service charges on deposit accounts, no loan commitment fees, no balance deficiency fees, no charges for NSF and overdrafts. Fees had became an easy source of income and helped offset the ever-shrinking margin. If it moved, banks put a price on it! But there was a limit to the advantage fees provided.

The banks then determined that there was only one more place for them to attack: their operating expenses. They proceeded to cut costs wherever they could through across-the-board headcount reductions, sales of business units, closing branches, exiting markets, selling buildings, and consolidating operations. Most of the banks had built up huge infrastructures over the years, thinking that they would always be able to afford them.

An article published in mid-1988 carried a headline that read, "All Over the World, Banks Are Cutting Costs!" Since then, there have been some enormous cost reduction efforts in the financial services industry. The headlines say it all:

- First Bank System's New Chairman Swings Ax and Tightens Purse Strings
- Citicorp to Cut 4,250 Jobs over Two Years
- Chase to Offer Severance to Employees, Take a $30 Million 3rd-Quarter Charge
- Fleet/Norstar to Cut 5% of Work Force
- Ameritrust to Lay Off 780 in Move to Cut Expenses
- Shawmut Posts Quarterly Loss, Will Cut Staff

- This Time the Downturn Is Dressed in Pinstripes
- Same Song, Second Verse at 1st Insterstate

And there were many, many more. Banks were becoming concerned about their cost structures and began to take some radical actions.

ONE BANK'S STORY: THE RIF (REDUCTION IN FORCE) AT U.S. BANCORP

U.S. Bancorp in Portland (Oregon) completed a corporate restructuring in 1985 that reduced staff and noninterest expense by 10 percent.[14] The bank had not been under any particular cost pressures as its earnings were average. In late October 1985, executive management of U.S. Bancorp determined that a staffing reduction program was necessary. They asked their management staff to determine the positions within their areas that could be eliminated or consolidated. By mid-November, they had an initial target of 600 positions. The targets were not set completely from the bottom-up; Dan Sullivan, the controller, indicated that he was given a goal of 25 percent of his staff.

In early November, Chairman John Elorriaga sent a letter to the employees saying that there were to be organizational changes throughout the bank by way of consolidation and elimination of functions. The letter also stated the need for staff reductions. Their goal was to achieve the reduction through attrition and a special retirement program, but the potential for terminations was presented clearly in the chairman's letter.

The reaction to this announcement was one of shock and surprise. Rumors about the staff reduction started, and, as is normal, exaggerated the potential number of staff reductions. People all over the bank began to get nervous.

An overview committee, chaired by Earl Livengood, the auditor, was assembled to review the lists of people to be displaced. All selections for the list had to be fair and non-discriminatory, with the notification of those to be displaced coming in December, continuing into January, only 2½ months after the decision to downsize had been made. Letters were sent to those to be terminated.

By mid-January, 50 displaced staff members had found other jobs in the company; 250 had resigned or been terminated; and another 200 had taken the special retirement package. The total RIF was about 10 percent of the workforce.

Management wanted to make sure that those who were displaced were treated fairly so they established a Career Transition Center; hired a local outplacement firm to hold seminars on how to locate employment; and created a new severance package that included benefits. Many banks would not have gone that far.

With the RIF completed, the bank believed that hiring and other related employment activities would be almost nonexistent in 1986. They were in for a surprise. In early February 1986, the employment area of human resources began to get busy, and by the end of the month, internal job postings had reached 1985 levels. In March and April, internal postings were greater than 1985 levels and external hiring was twice the 1985 level.

A GOOD EXAMPLE OF "COST CREEP"

What happened at U.S. Bancorp was a prime example of "cost creep." Without knowing the value of the services represented by the expenses, the bank did not know which were the right ones to take out. Otto Becker, managing partner of Ernst & Young's Great Lakes Consulting Practice, observes that, "What they [the banks] don't realize is that 85 percent to 90 percent of these costs will be back within two or three years."[15] In fact, "The cost reduction effort has failed because the symptom of the problem, growth in support personnel, has been attacked, but the fundamental causes remain. The plant is still being asked to produce the same diversity and complexity of outputs that generated the demand for support personnel."[16]

This very quick return to the previous hiring level created morale problems and defeated the financial purpose of the RIF, not to mention the damage the bank did to its ability to service customers. Many employees saw this as an indication that the RIF had not been necessary—which was, in fact, the case. Management had not considered the value to the customer of the activities being performed by the people to be displaced, and since the demand did not slacken, the people had to be brought back on.

As the effects of the RIF lingered at U.S. Bancorp, managers were faced with a lack of internal applicants for their openings; employees seemed to want to stay put, in the safety of their current positions. Valerie White of the Employee Services area called this "Survivor Syndrome," which is characterized by keeping one's head down, never taking any risk, being afraid of making a mistake, not trying anything new and different, and having a general lack of innovation.

The RIF in 1985 was not an atypical exercise. It was short-term, swift and decisive, very unpleasant, and, in the long run, unsuccessful. The bank did not change the structure of the ways work was divided and coordinated. Hundreds of banks all over the country did the same thing. The results were predictable, because the "slash-and-burns" missed the value represented by the costs that were being cut out. However, that was all that they knew how to do.

THE ERNST & YOUNG/NABCA SURVEY

As the 1980s came to a close, the financial services industry was still in serious trouble. Deregulation had come too late, and many bankers did not know how to respond to the sudden opportunity to be able to compete on the basis of cost and price. Asset quality was a continuing problem for them; rumors of mergers surfaced daily; but cost reduction was the main concern. Banks simply had to improve their earnings and capital bases, and with the margin being squeezed and limited opportunities for increasing fee income, the expense base was the generally accepted answer.

The National Association for Bank Cost and Management Accounting (NABCA) was also concerned about rising costs and devoted its annual convention in the summer of 1990 to a program aimed at value creation in the financial services industry. For that convention, a questionnaire was sent to the association's membership of just over 400 banks of all sizes. Over 20 percent of the members, 81 banks, responded. The objectives were to determine if these banks had undertaken a cost reduction program, what their strategies had been, and how successful they were. Specific questions about various structural issues were included.

The survey confirmed that cost management was a new but popular activity. Eighty-five percent of the respondents indicated that they had undertaken a cost reduction effort within the previous three years, suggesting that they were just beginning to react to earnings pressures on the expense side of the income statement. Of them, average noninterest expense savings was 8.3 percent—a poor showing in light of the 30 percent put forth in Chapter 3 as the cost of poor quality. Only four of the responding banks, or less than 5 percent of the sample, reported that they had realized savings of more than 10 percent. Fifteen of the banks whose cost reduction projects were still underway predicted they would get savings of over 17 percent; this seemed optimistic compared to actual results. Fully 70 percent of the banks reported that they had achieved, or were going to achieve, savings *of less than 5 percent*! That is a small amount when considering all of the time and effort that has gone into the project, so much so that one must question whether there were any real savings at all.

Banks used and were using the following approaches to accomplish their cost reductions:

Action	Project Completed	Project in Progress
Eliminate/downsize departments	88%	87%
Consolidate operations	82%	75%
Process improvement	82%	73%
Consolidate branches	59%	62%
Reduce expenses across-the-board	53%	42%
Increase capacity utilization	47%	46%
Sell business lines	41%	64%
Quality control	29%	62%
Employee suggestions	29%	67%
Reduce headcount across-the-board	29%	29%
Value engineering	6%	14%

The most common tactic was to eliminate departments and to consolidate operations and branches. These were the easiest to accomplish and promised short-term economic benefit, but without consideration of the value that was being removed, were likely the wrong approaches and setting the stage for cost creep. What is interesting is that banks that were planning to reduce costs or were in the process of reducing costs projected far greater usage of quality improvement techniques such as quality control, employee suggestions, and value engineering than most banks actually used. In other words, when push came to shove, the banks opted for the slash-and-burn over value creation.

The structural findings were similarly counterproductive. On average, there were six levels of management between the top and bottom of the organization (the average was four, for banks $9 billion and less, and eight for those greater than $10 billion), and as many as 10 and 15 in the larger banks. Compare that with Federal Express. With over 92,000 employees worldwide, it has no more than five levels of management anywhere in the company.

A very small number of banks said they used value engineering techniques. It is a new concept in which the bank determines customer demand and required quality levels, and then reorganizes its delivery systems to provide the expected service. This is why the issue of structure is important. Value engineering keys off customer demand and then flattens structures and streamlines processes, reallocating potentially displaced resources to areas where demand is high.

Most of the banks' projects were expense productivity exercises that will not have the desired long-term results. In fact, "a bank that concentrates all its efforts on productivity improvement is likely to see the quality of its service decline, which over the longer-term will lead to more lost customers and more poor-quality work needing to be redone. The ultimate result is a loss, not a gain in productivity and a rise in costs."[17]

The results reported by banks that had completed their projects were mediocre. Average noninterest expense reduction was 6.4 percent, and average full-time equivalent reduction was 5.1 percent. Banks with projects underway were more optimistic about their anticipated results, but they were still a lackluster 9 and 8 percent reduction, respectively. Based on the performance of those who had already finished, they were probably overestimating NIE reduction by 29 percent, and FTE reduction by 36 percent. Such small gains would be wiped out by inflation alone in a year or two.

The industry was in a state of shock. Asset quality needed to be reestablished; existing capacity had to be reduced or utilized; costs were soaring. The banks needed a new philosophy, one based on the longer view of meeting customer demand with high quality services, with organizations dedicated to these goals, in order to establish themselves as competitive forces once again.

NOTES

1. Tom Harvey worked at Union Commerce Bank from 1977 to 1983, prior to its acquisition by Huntington Bank.

2. Catherine Yang, et al., "The Future of Banking," *Business Week*, April 22, 1991, p. 75.

3. Donald Rataczek, "Too Many Banks and Too Little Capital: What This Means for the Economic Recovery," speech presented to the National Association of Bank Cost and Management Accounting, March 20, 1991.

4. "Foreign Banks Keep Stepping Up Their Siege," *Business Week*, June 3, 1991, p. 20.

5. Interview with David S. Hanick, chief financial officer, National City Bank, Cleveland, Ohio, February 25, 1991.

6. Ron Chernow, *The House of Morgan* (New York: Atlantic Monthly Press, 1990), p. 323.

7. Edwin Green, *Banking* (New York: Rizzoli Publications, 1989), p. 113.

8. Chernow, *House of Morgan*, p. 366.

9. Carter H. Golembe, "Special Constraints on Commercial Banks—Geographic Limitations," in *The Banker's Handbook*, ed. William H. Baughn, Thomas I. Storrs, and Charles E. Walker (Homewood, Ill., Dow Jones-Irwin 1988), p. 89.

10. Greg Lunde of Polycentric Strategies, Inc., from the April 16, 1991, letter accompanying his report to the Bank of North Dakota.

11. Ron Suskind, "New England Banker, Sticking to Old Ways, Avoided Rivals' Woes," *Wall Street Journal*, February 19, 1991, p. A1.

12. This chapter and Figure 2.4 are from Greg Lunde's report for the Bank of North Dakota, August 1986. Used by permission.

13. The Bank of North Dakota is an agency of the state government, established to promote agriculture, commerce, and industry within North Dakota. Its depositors and stockholders are the citizens of North Dakota. The bank's principal source of funds are state deposits.

14. Tom Harvey was a manager with Society Corporation at this time and spearheaded a project to research cost reduction strategies for the bank. He met with John Kinman, corporate director of human resources, who arranged interviews with the people in human resources who were responsible for the day-to-day operation of the RIF; the chairman of the RIF overview committee, Earl Livengood; and Dan Sullivan, the controller.

15. Interview with Otto Becker, managing partner, Ernst & Young's Great Lakes Consulting Practice, September 16, 1990.

16. H. Thomas Johnson and Robert S. Kaplan, *Relevance Lost: The*

Rise and Fall of Management Accounting (Boston: Harvard Business School Press, 1987), p. 244.

17. Clifford D. Moore, III, and David B. Peters, "Measuring/Auditing the Quality of Bank Service," *Journal of Bank Accounting and Auditing* (Fall 1987): 35.

Chapter 3

Quality Improvement Is the Answer

If cutting staff, selling assets, and merging with competitors don't solve the problems, then what will? The answer has its roots in the Bell Laboratories of the 1930s, and comes back to us in the 1990s by way of Japan. It is said that there is a correlation between an idea's "seepage" and its ultimate longevity. If so, the "new" solution should be with us a very long time. Indeed, consumers can only hope it will become the dominant impetus for most organizations' actions.

The answer, of course, is quality. Whether it is defined as "conformance to specifications,"[1] "fitness for use," "freedom from deficiencies,"[2] or even the generally maligned "I know it when I see it" that most of us secretly subscribe to, it is deservedly if belatedly the hottest word in business today. This chapter briefly traces the history of the quality movement and describes three of the seminal and dominant thinkers in the field: W. Edwards Deming, Joseph Juran, and Philip Crosby. It will point out some common threads, and discuss what implications the theories have for financial institutions. Finally, it will touch on the Malcolm Baldrige National Quality Award, although a full discussion of that subject is reserved for Chapter 8.

HISTORY OF THE QUALITY MOVEMENT

The Bell Laboratories of the 1930s must have been an exciting place to work. All kinds of innovative research was taking place there, and none was more important than the work of a statistician named Walter Shewhart. Shewhart developed the process control chart, and made the revelatory distinction between "special causes" of variations in processes, those that could be tackled directly, and "common causes," which could be reduced, though not eliminated, only by changing the process itself. Another Bell Labs researcher, W. Edwards Deming, took this work one step farther and developed a method of measuring variations and distinguishing between the two basic causes. His research led to "statistical process control" (SPC), which, in its applied form, enabled managers—generally manufacturing foremen—to ignore the normal deviations and concentrate on eliminating the special, controllable variations.

Statistical process control was an instant hit in the business world, but died a quick death as World War II boosted demand for manufactured goods to incredible levels that assured prosperity and largely obviated the need for controlling scrap, waste, and other costs of quality. It was easier and just as profitable then to inspect defects out rather than build quality in. Another cause of the demise, according to Deming, was the lack of commitment by top management. By the end of World War II, statistical process control was all but dead in America.

In contrast, it was resurrected with increased vigor in Japan. That economy, devastated rather than enriched by the war, had two obstacles to surmount: relatively low productivity and a reputation for poor quality. As part of the postwar reconstruction of Japan, a number of Bell Labs employees, including Deming, became involved with tackling some of the manufacturing problems faced by Japanese companies. Deming didn't make the same mistake twice. Although SPC was technically oriented, he ensured that commitment from management was part of the process.

The Japanese made a number of innovations to the basic

statistical process control method, innovations that led to the concept of total quality management. Some of these include: top management commitment; quality circles; quality training for all levels and functions; continuous quality improvement and seemingly impossibly high standards; and company-wide quality control (CWQC). Deming was the quality king in Japan, and in 1951 the Deming Prize was established as a very prestigious award for total quality.

Only 29 years later, in 1980, America rediscovered Deming, in a program aired by NBC called "If Japan Can . . . Why Can't We?" which portrayed the great strides that Japan had made in the quality of their products and the almost fanatical standards to which they adhere. With some American firms having lost significant ground to the Japanese and others facing stiff competition, SPC and the Deming method were re-embraced by the United States.

The year before this, however, another voice was heard to say that "Quality is free," and to assert that the cost of poor quality is higher than the cost of building quality in the first time. As a corporate vice president at ITT, Philip Crosby saved that company $720 million by implementing a zero-defects quality program. His was a bottom-up program, focused largely on who will ultimately have to do the job. Crosby was a true practitioner, more concerned with developing tools that work than theories to wrap around them.

Joseph Juran, another of the Bell Labs prodigies, was a statistician and theorist. He viewed quality as a business strategy and tended to work from the top down. He maintained that quality is *not* free, but that an investment of time and money is necessary to diagnose the causes of poor quality and remedy them.

Being statistically grounded, most of the quality work in America has been in the manufacturing sector and is only slowly spilling into services. Even then, the focus has been on customer service which, important as it is, is only one piece of the quality puzzle. Back-office operations, internal services, structure, culture, and costs must all be encompassed.

W. EDWARDS DEMING AND
STATISTICAL PROCESS CONTROL (SPC)

The ultimate goal of SPC is to provide more jobs. It achieves this by improving quality, which necessarily decreases costs, increases productivity, and grabs more market share for the company doing it. This is the Deming chain reaction, and it's a very powerful concept. It sounds a little like "enlightened self-interest," which also motivates organizations to do the right thing for somewhat selfish although not necessarily wrong reasons. The customer is explicitly considered in this equation, as grabbing more market share really means attracting more customers. The customer is also included in the Deming flow diagram (see Figure 3.1), where the defining and redefining of customer needs lead to adaptation and innovation in products (and services), leading to changes in inputs, processes, and finally outputs, which starts the flow all over again.

Statistical process control works by measuring the variations in a process enough times to get it to a stable state. Once

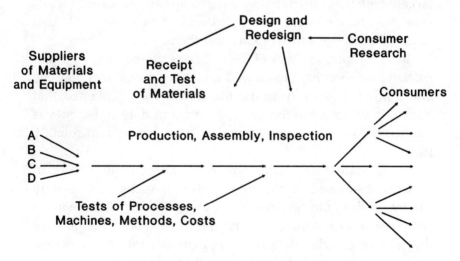

Figure 3.1. Deming Flow Diagram

this state has been reached, the goal of SPC is twofold: to reduce special causes of variations and to reduce the upper and
lower limits of acceptable normal variation. Although primarily
manufacturing-related, it can be applied to any process that is
measurable, and virtually any process is. The only problem
with SPC is that it requires constant tracking and charting to be
effective, which takes enormous discipline and commitment.

Deming supplements SPC with broad organizational pre-
scriptions that can be adapted for and applied to individual
companies. With a strong emphasis on worker empowerment,
the 14 Points, as he calls them, are essentially cultural directives
targeting senior management in order to incite revolutionary
cultural changes. They are as follows:

1. Create constancy of purpose toward improvement of
   products and services, with the aim of becoming competitive, staying in business, and providing jobs.
2. Adopt the new philosophy. We are in a new economic
   age. Western management must awaken to the challenge, learn their responsibilities, and take on leadership for change.
3. Cease reliance on mass inspection to achieve quality.
   Eliminate the need for inspection on a mass basis by
   building quality into the product in the first place.
4. End the practice of awarding business on the basis of
   price tag. Instead, minimize total cost. Move toward a
   single supplier for any one item, and establish a long-
   term relationship of loyalty and trust.
5. Improve constantly and forever the system of production and service, to improve quality and productivity,
   and thus constantly decrease costs.
6. Institute on-the-job training.
7. Institute leadership. The aim of supervision should be
   to help people, machines, and gadgets to do a better
   job. Supervision of management and production
   workers is in need of overhaul.

8. Drive out fear, so that everyone can work effectively for the company.

9. Break down barriers between departments. People in research, design, sales, and production must work as a team, to foresee problems of production and use that may be encountered with the product or service.

10. Eliminate slogans, exhortations, and targets for the workforce asking for zero defects and new levels of productivity. Such exhortations only create adversarial relationships, since the bulk of the causes of low quality and low productivity belong to the system and thus lie beyond the power of the workforce.

11a. Eliminate work standards (quotas) on the factory floor. Substitute leadership.

11b. Eliminate management by objectives. Eliminate management by numbers and numerical goals. Substitute leadership.

12a. Remove barriers that rob the hourly workers of their right to pride of workmanship. The responsibility of supervisors must be changed from mere numbers to quality.

12b. Remove barriers that rob people in management and in engineering of their right to pride of workmanship. This means, *inter alia,* abolishment of the annual review or merit-rating and of management by objectives.

13. Institute a vigorous program of education and self-improvement.

14. Put everybody in the company to work to accomplish the transformation. The transformation is everybody's job.

Deming warns against 7 Deadly Diseases that prevent a quality orientation in a company. These include the MBA style of management with its focus on numbers and short-term results, as well as performance measurement systems such as management by objectives and performance appraisals. Deming prefers to foster teamwork instead. He is fond of quoting a fellow statistician, Lloyd Nelson, who says that "The most important figures needed for management of any organization are unknown and unknowable."[3] Since most problems are management-controllable not worker-controllable, it makes little sense to Deming to hold individuals accountable; besides, as the Japanese learned, it takes everyone working together to really make quality work.

JOSEPH W. JURAN

Juran elevated quality from an operational process to a strategic initiative alongside finance, marketing, sales, and other areas of strategic planning. The Juran Trilogy, in fact, directly parallels financial management, outlining three levels of quality management: quality planning, which is customer-based; quality control; and quality improvement. The final goal is complete freedom from deficiencies, which is the Juran definition of quality. There are two quality journeys, diagnostic and remedial, and in the triple role (or TRIPROL) of Juran, everyone is customer, processor, and supplier.[4] Therefore, it is essential to cross functional and organizational lines to get to the true nature of the quality problem and, therefore, its solution.

Juran differentiates between Big Quality, which is company-wide and comprehensive, and Little Quality, which is aimed at specific areas and projects. Generally, it is practical to do lots of Little Qs in order to achieve the Big Q; knowing which ones to do is made easier by the Pareto process he pioneered, which enables organizations to prioritize projects and distinguish the "vital few from the useful many."

Juran emphasizes the radical cultural change that will have to occur in an organization, and he establishes clear management roles and responsibilities. To get through an entire strategic quality management cycle takes five to six years—not a minor undertaking.

QUALITY IS FREE

ITT was one organization that undertook to shape a culture of quality, and it began the process in 1965 by installing Philip Crosby at the head of their quality management program. His work with ITT led to the publication of *Quality Is Free* (1979), which became instant "must read" material for all managers and supervisors. In it, he developed the concepts of making quality certain and zero defects. Quality, for him, is defined as "conformance to requirements" as measured by the cost of "unquality," or nonconformance.

Similar to Deming, Crosby develops 14 cultural and practical steps for implementing a quality program. They establish quality councils, as well as celebration of a Zero Defects Day. The crux of Crosby's philosophy is that high quality costs an organization nothing, because the benefits of quality outweigh the investment to achieve it. In the dedication of his book to Harold S. Geneen, he quotes Geneen as saying, "Quality is not only right, it is free. And it is not only free, it is the most profitable product line we have."[5]

COMMON THREADS

Four themes run through each of these quality proponents' thinking:

1. *Quality is a cultural change.* It is not a quick fix, and it is not easy. It is not particularly compatible with many current organizational forms and practices. It requires a new way of thinking, problem-solving, working together, and rewarding.

2. *Quality starts at the top.* Cultural changes can be directed only from one place: the top. The responsibility for problems belongs to management. Eighty to 85 percent of the problems are caused by or can only be solved by management.[6] All the worker empowerment in the world

will be for nothing if management doesn't assume its own responsibility first.

3. *Management commitment is essential.* Obviously if the responsibility is management's, the commitment to change must derive from there as well. The key word is "commitment"—long-term, unwavering, upheld-even-when-third-quarter-profits-are-down commitment. Employees are ever alert to signs of the demise of the fad of the month. Quality must be more than that. It must be *the* way of doing business.

4. *Quality is a profit strategy.* There is no choice to be made between quality and profitability. Improving quality is the cheapest way to increase profits. In today's financial services environment, where new product advantage lasts about a day, it may be the only way.

QUALITY IN BANKING

There have been significant steps taken toward achieving quality in banking and some excellent books written on the subject, such as *Service Quality: A Profit Strategy for Financial Institutions* by Len Berry et al. and *Quality Management in Financial Services* by Chuck Aubrey. These books describe the costs associated with poor service, in terms of market share loss and consequently increased marketing expenditures, employee turnover and the associated expense, and the loss of pricing flexibility. They compellingly illustrate the point that service is really all that banks have to sell; that it is the only means of differentiating themselves; and that it is the *sine qua non* of progressive, leading financial institutions. In one of these books, John G. Medlin, Jr., chairman, president, and chief executive officer of First Wachovia Corporation, is quoted as saying, "Quality service is one of the few ways a financial institution can differentiate itself sufficiently in the marketplace to achieve exceptional business growth and earnings performance. It can help cut costs and boost revenues through relationship broadening, productivity enhancement, and error reduction. Therefore, service quality is a key element of our profit strategy."[7]

But service quality is only one component of a total quality program. Quality in banking must go beyond smiling tellers who make eye contact and use customers' names. Banking quality consists of three components: internal excellence, effectiveness, and efficiency; superior customer service; and an organization structure that is designed explicitly to support the quality orientation. The growth of poor service and poor quality can be traced to the structural and environmental or cultural roots; conversely, these organizational elements must inevitably manifest themselves in poor internal and external service. All of these components are inextricably intertwined; "fixing" them will lead directly to greater pricing flexibility, increased market share, and, ultimately, higher profitability.

Quality must be built into all the products and services a bank produces; it must be the driving force of its internal processes; it must permeate even the structure and design of the organization, both the formal and informal lines of communication and authority. Only then will tellers have something to smile about. Only then will the customer be truly served.

Some American banks have introduced many features of quality management into their operations. Certainly parts of the back-office operations are obvious candidates for statistical process control. There is little difference between manufacturing production lines and check-processing production lines in terms of proofing, sorting, storing, statementing, and mailing. Yet there are banks that don't measure their defect rates in these and other processing areas.

Most banks have introduced customer service training for their tellers and platform officers, especially in the retail area. Peak-time teller staffing is a part of this effort, as is sales training. These programs have had successes, but too often these measures are limited to the branches and not integrated with back-office procedure or management objectives. Tellers are evaluated in terms of fast, efficient transaction service, friendly and personal relationship banking, and the cross-selling of products to new and existing customers. These are often mutually exclusive performance criteria, yet tellers are evaluated on all of them and rewarded accordingly.

Even banks that have an excellent service program have often been unable or unwilling to import their ideals to the rest of the organization, particularly to the staff areas. The retail bank of Security Pacific National Bank, for instance, has a comprehensive quality program for its branch employees and some service agreements with Security Pacific Automation Company, its data-processing support. Yet there is very little carryover into the business bank or to the staff support functions. Although there are hundreds of "service level agreements" in effect between internal users and providers of services, these are not tied to any integrated quality management program. In fact, it is a surprise to many Security Pacific employees outside the branches to learn that there is a quality program.

Dale Ruby, a senior vice president and head of the retail bank quality program, struggles daily with the question of whether Security Pacific is too big to have all-inclusive quality management. He cites the geographic dispersion of the bank, the many layers of management, the various management teams, and compartmentalization as problems in communicating the quality message throughout the entire organization. Will it one day be disseminated farther than the retail bank? Says Ruby, "I have to believe it will be, because it's the right thing to do." For now, "I don't have time to convince everyone else that they should be on the same bandwagon."[8]

In 1990 Society Corporation, a large regional bank headquartered in Cleveland, Ohio, had an opportunity to attack its cost of quality in a major way. Tom Harvey was then a vice president at Society in charge of financial performance improvement strategies. Harvey had learned that "30% of noninterest expense is related to doing things wrong or to things that did not have to be done at all,"[9] and had calculated that applying—conservatively—half that percentage to Society's noninterest expense and tax affecting the product resulted in a cost of quality of $52 million! All Society had to do was find out what the customers wanted and the quality level they expected and then redesign the organization and delivery processes to do only those things. Not only would they reap huge financial benefits, but the pain of an across-the-board reduction would be avoided. Nevertheless, Society, as most banks, chose to implement an expense productivity program in the guise of a value-added activity study.

This speaks volumes about the state of quality in our banks. It certainly goes a long way toward explaining why the independent banks, much smaller than the New York money center or large regional banks, are running circles around the big banks in terms of service quality. And it has ominous implications for the future of the industry, which is expected to shrink and consolidate, resulting in fewer and larger banks. On the other hand, it appears to point to a tremendous opportunity for the independent banks, and perhaps indicates that they have less to fear than they think from encroachment by deregulated, interstate megabanks.

COMMITTED TO QUALITY

A few banks have taken the total quality management approach. It is important to look at what they're doing, why they have the commitment when so many banks do not, and what the results of their programs have been. Three banks committed to quality are First Tennessee Bank in Memphis; BancOne of Ohio; and MBNA America (formerly Maryland Bank), the Newark, Delaware, credit card company. The common threads in each of these stories are the active commitment of top management to quality; an integrated, company-wide approach; and the eventual assimilation of quality into the culture of the organization.

First Tennessee Bank

First Tennessee Bank is a $7.4 billion bank headquartered in Memphis, Tennessee.[10] Its quality program dates back to the early 1980s and encompasses a wide variety of programs and initiatives. The chief executive, Ron Terry, is given credit for instigating the quality system program; First Tennessee managers credit him with the recognition that quality is a strategic element in the overall business plan for the bank. It was up to senior management to spread that vision, and ultimately to disseminate it into individual groups. First Tennessee managers take a dim view of the likelihood of success for a company that does not have absolute, unwavering top management commitment.

The program was initially implemented on two fronts, operational and managerial. First, statistical process control was implemented in the back office, including defining goals and upper and lower variation limits and establishing and training task forces to tackle problems. At the same time, all senior managers were sent to Philip Crosby's quality school in Florida; a Quality Council, comprised of senior managers, was formed; and a separate, independent group called Quality Systems was created, which was to report directly to the chairman. Ron Terry is always careful to pick a recognized successful performer to head Quality Systems. Later, formal team-building was begun to open communication channels between functions and divisions and to lessen internal competition among them. There is a very strong focus on customer satisfaction, and telephone surveys measuring six areas of quality have been conducted annually since 1987. They also make extensive use of internal telephone shoppers and external face-to-face shoppers. In 1991 they began to formally use benchmarking techniques, measuring themselves against their competitors. Internally, a survey called the Employee Quality Index is administered once or twice a year.

The program implemented tremendous cultural change, but now quality has truly been enculturated. Ron Terry still talks about quality, quality planning shows up on the corporate calendar along with financial and strategic planning, and quality measures are a key part of the performance appraisal and bonus system (20 to 25 percent of managers' annual bonuses depends on quality measures and their implementation of their quality plan). Quality is part of their recruiting process: Potential employees are screened for their attitudes toward service quality, and new people are sent through the same quality and team-building exercises that everyone else has gone through. It is so well engrained in the culture that new employees tend to absorb the right attitudes through osmosis; those who don't tend to leave the company, since it is not possible for them to be effective in their jobs. Quality really only needs to be managed now, and Quality Systems has been merged with a line unit and is administered for the entire corporation out of that area.

A number of reward programs reinforce the importance of quality to First Tennessee. They don't really believe in financial rewards, except for bonuses and some productivity incentives, but they have three highly visible and prestigious awards that are bestowed, not necessarily annually, but as earned. One is the Best Award, given to production units. Every unit meeting production standards over time is a candidate; the Best Award is then voted on by users. Another is the Excellence Award, which is earned by going above and beyond the call of duty in customer service. Candidates are nominated by either an external or internal customer, and the winner becomes eligible for the Chairman's Award. The Chairman's Award was established in the early 1980s, formalized in 1987–88, and was given for the first time only in 1990. This most prestigious and exclusive award recognizes the accomplishment of a project with excellent and financially significant results, demonstrating the relationship of quality to bottom-line profitability.

One of the best programs to come out of their formal quality program was the use of internal service contracts between users and providers. To change any internal process requires a lengthy review with users. For example, if the head of human resources wants to implement drug-testing, he puts together a review team, starting at lower organizational levels, including workers, and progressively going higher as bugs are worked out. Or, if a new product is being introduced, the product manager holds meetings with all affected personnel to tell them how the product will alter their jobs, to inform them of the support it needs, and to get their input. This is a mandated process, and it has a Japanese feel to it; it works more slowly, by consensus, then implements quickly and smoothly.

By 1988, First Tennessee felt confident and proud enough of their quality program that they applied for the Baldrige Award; this was the first year the award was in existence. (The Baldrige Award is introduced later in this chapter and discussed fully in Chapter 8.) They did not win the award—only one service company and no bank has won to date—but the fact that they felt able to apply so early testifies to their faith in themselves and their programs.

BancOne

BancOne is the classic example of a company that was motivated by a crisis to seize quality as the right way to do business in the future.[11] The crisis came in 1984, and their response was to attend a Deming seminar, which convinced them that they needed to have a full quality effort. In 1985 they hired a manager of quality and productivity improvement, who was to report to the chief financial officer. Eventually the title was changed to chief quality officer, and that position exists in each of BancOne's affiliate banks. Service quality is viewed as the cornerstone of a long-term profitability and productivity strategy.

Once the decision to pursue quality was made, the first step was to educate and train all 18,000 employees in the basic concepts of quality, including John McCoy, the chairman. The focus of the two-day workshops was on controlling and improving services, not just the how but also the why. Next, each bank conducted a training program for its employees, to teach them how to manage the quality of customer service. Although front-room quality measures are "fuzzy," they can be obtained via customer research, shopping the tellers, and tracking kinds and numbers of errors. The back room is more easily measured with standard statistical tools such as SPC and defect rates, and the processes are relatively easier to improve. At BancOne, though, teams are expected to find and close gaps in every area of customer service, to initiate improvement projects, and to get results. The measures are also part of the annual quality plan, as part of their overall strategy to achieve world-class, "legendary" customer service.

BancOne estimates its cost of quality at 25 percent of noninterest expense, which is being constantly reduced through its quality program. In 1990 alone, quality initiatives saved the bank $12 million; they average around $28,000 in savings per project in reduced manpower and decreased expenses. Increased revenue is the other, more positive side of the coin. As people become more experienced in recognizing and dealing with opportunities, the savings and revenue improvements may even increase, and "you never run out of improvement opportunities." They have learned that defects in any process cost them money, both in hard and soft dollars.

MBNA America

MBNA America started as Maryland Bank, National Association; what is now MBNA America was actually their credit card processing facility. In 1982, the 100-person facility was spun off to operate independently. It has pioneered the use of "affinity cards," credit cards offered to their members through various sponsoring groups such as alumni associations, special interest organizations, and professional groups. The cards are customized with a logo or picture identifying the sponsor affiliation. One whole wall in their facility displays the various cards—and they are really quite lovely.

There are two things that strike the visitor entering the lobby of the main building. First, the building is attractive and unbanklike. Second, there is a large rug that says, "The Customer First." A walk around the lobby reveals other quotations—painted above the door, framed over an award cabinet, hung in the guard area—that tout customer service. Some examples:

- 6,000 people and every one with an attitude . . . Satisfy the Customer.
- Think of yourself as a Customer. (This is above *every single* door in the facility.)
- This is the house the Customer and the people of MBNA built. Great people build great houses.
- Complacency is devastating.
- Take the Customer's point of view: Fix it right and fix it fast.
- TTT (Think Things Through)

All of this is impressive, to be sure, but it's difficult not to be a little skeptical.

MBNA America is a place that has to be seen to be believed. The sloganeering goes on and on, but it's sincere. And talking to various managers and other people—MBNA America doesn't like or use the word "employee"—it is clear that the banners are only the outward manifestation of a quality culture that is thoughtful, well planned, deeply ingrained, and highly successful. Bill Morrison, an executive vice president, once told a group of bankers from Omaha, "You can write down all the quotations and go back to Nebraska and paint them on your walls, but that won't achieve quality."

As it must be, the driving force for customer satisfaction is the chairman, Charles Cawley. He is consistently given credit for the culture, attitude, and climate that focus attention on people and customers. The climate permeates everything about MBNA America: leadership, hiring ("people who like people"), internal surveys (when we were there one was being distributed by the facilities people regarding gardening and plant maintenance), cleanliness, education ("you train your dog, you educate people"[12]), cafeteria food, fitness facilities, quality planning. The message is consistent and undeniably upbeat.

MBNA America views regulation as an easy excuse for banks not to provide service, and deregulation as an opportunity to find out what the customer really wants. They realize that if banks aren't careful, there may not be a need for them.

Their strategy appears to be twofold: (1) get people excited about their jobs and let that translate into superior customer service; and (2) have an unrelenting attitude toward customer satisfaction. In *Reinventing the Corporation*, the authors quote New Hope Communication as saying that they will only do business with people who are pleasant.[13] MBNA America has a similar attitude; a manager from Bank Group Marketing, Steve Shepherd, stated that "MBNA has high quality and low cost and the best customer service. If a bank doesn't want that, we don't want them for a customer."

THE INDEPENDENT BANKS

Despite the concerns of the independent banks—the country's smaller banks, having generally less than $1 billion in assets—about the effects of proposed deregulation on their ability to compete with super-regional banks, as a group they are faring much better than their bigger counterparts. Financially they are much more successful: the NABCA survey (discussed in Chapter 2) showed that the return on assets (ROA) of all banks is around 1.1 percent; community banks report average ROA of 1.4 percent. Their ratings in terms of customer service are consistently higher. Is it just, as Dale Ruby of SPNB suggests, a matter of size?

The answer appears to be both yes and no. Yes, size does make a difference, but no, because it is more how the larger size translates into service, or lack of it, rather than sheer size alone. Focus groups consistently decry the impersonal nature of larger banks.[14] Many customers perceive that it is difficult to find the right person to handle transactions or solve problems, and they find people in large institutions to be generally rude and unwilling to acknowledge and fix mistakes. Interestingly, focus group customers said that tellers in large banks have these characteristics even when it was pointed out that they were likely to be local, just as the tellers in the independent banks. Nevertheless, there seemed to be something about the systems in place, the training, or the culture that caused the larger banks to be missing the warmth of the smaller banks.

Since the focus groups often go on to say that customer service is far more important than interest rates and service charges, it is clear that independent banks enjoy an advantage over their larger competitors. Unfortunately for many smaller banks, there are disadvantages that work against them, and these might be related to their size. Convenience is a problem for many independent banks. They simply don't have the resources to be everywhere, open as many hours, and have as many ATMs as the larger banks with their economies of scale.

Still, for many customers the attractions of being smaller and local give independent banks the edge over larger, nonlocal banks. To many, being local implies tradition, stability, roots, and familiarity. The smaller size gives people the sense that they can go to the top with their problems, if need be (regardless of whether that is actually true). Obviously, there are opportunities for both independent and larger banks. Independent banks need to find ways to make themselves more available to their customers, through expanded hours, greater networking, and perhaps more customized services. Larger banks need to make themselves more accessible to local customers who are accustomed to being treated as valued and important clients by their bankers.

THE MALCOLM BALDRIGE NATIONAL QUALITY AWARD

The Malcolm Baldrige National Quality Award, named for the late secretary of state, was signed into law by President Ronald Reagan in 1987. The purpose of the award is to recognize those companies that have accomplished excellence in quality, and to establish national awareness of quality as a goal and an achievement. Two awards may be given annually in each of three categories: manufacturing, small business, and services. Out of a possible 24 winners in 1988, 1989, 1990, and 1991, only 12 awards have been given. The first service award wasn't given until 1990, to Federal Express. No bank has ever won a Baldrige. Perhaps the closest any bank has come to winning is MBNA America, which received a site visit in 1990. The National Institute of Standards and Technology (NIST), the Department of Commerce agency that administers the Baldrige, does not track applications by industry, but it is estimated that half of all service sector applications come from banks.[15]

Certainly there is great and growing interest by banks in the Baldrige Award. Although the application is difficult and expensive, many are using the application for self-examination purposes, and some have structured their quality programs according to its criteria. Most discover in the process of applying that they are not ready to be judged in the world-class category. Of course, that is also true for most other companies. In 1991, 150,000 applications were mailed out but only 106 were completed and returned.

Banks that have been through the process, such as First Tennessee, are convinced of the value of the application process, regardless of the outcome. Self-discovery and the critique of an outside examining committee are cited as the two main benefits. The biggest problem for banks that want to apply is meeting the challenge of showing demonstrable results from their quality programs. A minimum of three years' worth of data is necessary for trending purposes; it is estimated that it takes at least three years to put all the processes of a quality program in place. Most banks have not been at the quality game that long, if they are playing at all.

Nevertheless, the application alone provides excellent guidelines for designing a long-term quality improvement program. It will surely point out the strengths and weaknesses in the organization, and give management some idea of what to expect in terms of commitment, time, and resources to put a program in place. To get assistance in ideas for improving quality, interested banks can contact former Baldrige winners (one of the stipulations of the competition is that the winners will share information about their own quality improvement practices). Even though no bank has successfully applied for the Baldrige as yet, many of the practices are transferable across industries.

BANKS AND THE QUALITY STRATEGY

Why haven't more banks adopted the quality strategy? It may be useful to look at the profit strategy spectrum (see Figure 3.2). Banks enjoyed a near-monopoly on financial services for several decades, even though there were some services that they were barred from providing. As a regulated industry, their profit margins were assured unless they did something really stupid.

After deregulation, banks were forced to employ another strategy: "If it moves, put a price on it." The fees angered customers, who saw no added value in services that had been given free for years and years, but they did help prop up falling

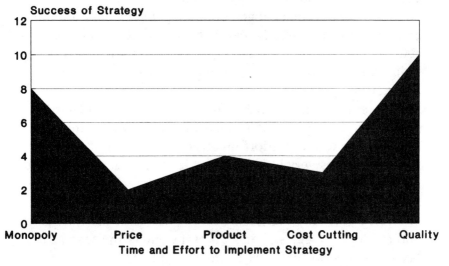

Figure 3.2. Profit Strategy Spectrum

earnings in a very substantial way. Unfortunately, disinter-mediation continued apace, as banking customers, feeling used and betrayed, moved their accounts to special investment ac-counts with check-writing privileges. The next step in the price wars was, then, to *eliminate* fees, which led to a plethora of new accounts, each with its own set of rules and restrictions. This profit strategy continues to be followed today, generally con-fusing consumers and adding to the training and marketing woes of banks.

The product strategy was followed for a time, but it is gen-erally agreed that the new product advantage now lasts a mat-ter of days, if not hours—hardly enough time to capture a market. Still, not developing new products is a sure way to get left behind, so this strategy, too, is still pursued.

The real news in banking, however, was cost-cutting. This venerable, hierarchical, bureaucratic institution suddenly found itself loaded with middle managers, excess capacity, huge staff groups, and all kinds of subsidiary businesses sheltered under its corporate umbrellas. The imperative in the 1970s and early 1980s, in many regions, to build branches every couple of blocks or so resulted in a double whammy in the late 1980s: too many people and too much real estate. And the eventual popularity of the automatic teller machine simply made most of those branches unnecessary. So began rounds and rounds of cost-cutting. Not many of these attempts were effective. The banking industry in general, however, is still clinging to cost-cutting as its profit strategy of choice.

This still doesn't answer the question of why. In Figure 3.2 the Y axis is the probable success of the strategy, while the X axis is the amount of effort involved in pursuing it. Having a monopoly takes very little effort but it is highly successful. The pricing and product strategies take more effort, and have lost most of their effectiveness today. Reducing cost takes quite a lot of effort but is only marginally more successful than the price and product strategies. Quality is at the end of the spectrum. It takes a whole lot of work to instill a quality culture into an organization that has never had it, and that partially explains why banks have so far been reluctant to undertake a *total* quality approach.

Yet it is the most successful of the strategies by far. It is obvious why that should be so: Quality will subsume the other four strategies, in time. Making quality the number one priority, and giving all employees the tools to pursue it, will almost automatically ensure that costs are lowered and innovative new products are created. These, coupled with excellent customer service, will permit greater pricing flexibility and greater market share. While no one can hope for a monopoly these days, a bank can create a monopoly-like situation in its own niche or region.

One of the reasons most banks have not opted for the quality strategy is due to the amount of work involved, though few would put it that way. Instead, they would decry the disruption, the loss of productivity, the time required. These are not trivial protests. Implementing a good quality program does take time, probably will disrupt the organization psychologically as well as physically, and may result in lowered productivity in some areas in the short term. But the protests point out another cause of rejecting the quality strategy: the undesirability of long-term gains if they require short-term pain.

Many bankers will say that their situation makes it necessary for them to choose between a quality strategy and a profit strategy. But quality *is* a profit strategy. While the bank that is facing imminent bankruptcy may be justified in pursuing short-term financial objectives, no other bank has that luxury.

Another obstacle that most banks need to overcome is the baggage of their traditional culture, which has given them a hierarchical, top-heavy management structure and a bureaucratic organizational style. It is extremely difficult to dismantle authority structures and empower both managers and workers to be innovative, motivated, independent thinkers and doers. Banks are even likely not to have the kind of people on board to make that transition easily. That doesn't mean it can't be made, however, and bankers are clearly among the brightest and best—if not the most creative—businesspeople of all industries.

The bottom line for most bankers is simple: They want quality, they recognize its potential, but they don't know how to start. They think it's complicated and technical, costly and, above all, unknown. As Juran says, "The 'supercause' of poor quality is a lack of a systematic, structured approach to quality management."[16] *Quality Value Banking* provides that approach.

NOTES

1. Philip B. Crosby, *Quality Is Free* (New York: McGraw Hill Book Company, 1979), p. 15.

2. Joseph M. Juran, *Juran on Leadership for Quality: An Executive Handbook* (New York: Free Press, 1989), pp. 15–16. ′

3. Henry R. Neave, "Deming Is Different," *The Quality Management Forum*, Volume 17, Number 1 (Spring 1991):3.

4. MBNA America in Newark, Delaware, takes that literally with signs all over their facility that exhort people to "Think of yourself as the Customer."

5. Crosby, *Quality Is Free*, dedication to H. S. G.

6. Deming says 85 percent of problems are management's, not workers', while Juran states that 80 percent of nonconformance is manager-controllable. Roger Milliken, chairman and CEO of Milliken & Co., a 1989 Baldrige Award winner, noted at the 1990 National Quality Forum that there are three obstacles to implementing quality: top management, middle management, and lower management.

7. Leonard L. Berry, David R. Bennett, and Carter W. Brown, *Service Quality: A Profit Strategy for Financial Institutions* (New York: Dow Jones-Irwin, 1989), p. 7.

8. Dale Ruby, interview at Security Pacific National Bank, Los Angeles, April 8, 1991.

9. Speech by Michael Hanson, J. D. Carreker & Associates, Inc., October 28, 1987.

10. This section is based on a telephone interview with G. Robert Vezina, senior vice president and head of human resources, and Rod White, vice president, First Tennessee Bank, March 19, 1991.

11. This section is based on an interview with Chuck Aubrey, chief quality officer, BancOne Corporation, February 4, 1991.

12. Craig Schroeder, vice president, MBNA America, quoting Charles M. Cawley, May 7, 1991.

13. John Naisbitt and Patricia Aburdene, *Reinventing the Corporation* (New York: Warner Books, 1985), p. 40.

14. Focus group study conducted by John Zogby Group International, Inc., for the Savings Bank of Utica, Utica, New York, 1991. Findings used by permission.

15. Chuck Aubrey of BancOne, Aubrey is also a Baldrige examiner.

16. Juran, *Juran on Leadership*, p. 181.

Chapter 4

The Quality Value Engineering (QVE) Approach

There are four important ways in which QVE differs from quality methodologies that have gone before it, especially those directed at financial institutions.

First, QVE examines the cost of quality from a different viewpoint—in terms of cost drivers, rather than simply line item reductions. Second, organization is included as a component of quality. No other method makes organizing for quality one of its fundamental tenets, and yet without this component nothing really changes. Third, QVE views customer service as only one part of a quality program, not the alpha and the omega. Fourth, QVE ties it all back to financial performance improvement, directed at long-term results. In short, QVE digs into the fundamental workings of the organization and places a quality program at its core, not on its surface. It is simple, practical, and profound.

WHAT IS QUALITY VALUE ENGINEERING?

What does "quality value engineering" mean? The simple answer is found by reading the term backward: *engineering*, directing, or managing the *value* of the bank through a strategy of *quality*. Another simple answer is that it is a systematic, structured approach to quality management. Quality Value Engineering is a detailed, thoughtful, comprehensive, yet essentially simple methodology that any bank can undertake to significantly improve the level of quality of its products, services, operations, and customer relations.

There are two ways to look at QVE: its conceptual framework and the practical "how to." The theoretical underpinnings of QVE will be discussed in this chapter, while the implementation of QVE will be the subject of Chapters 5, 6, and 7.

There are several dominant thinkers in the quality field—Deming, Juran, Crosby, and others not discussed—and numerous approaches, some of which, such as those developed by Berry and Aubrey, are specifically suited to financial institutions. QVE draws on the common threads identified in these theories, and takes the implementation a step or two farther than do its predecessors. For instance, Berry et al. provide an excellent methodology for identifying service gaps. But they are concerned only with customer service, and do not offer advice on what to do about those gaps. QVE is a total quality program that encompasses all the bank's operations and contains a problem-solving methodology.

The three major components of QVE are the cost of quality, organizing for quality, and quality customer service. If a bank covers these three bases, financial improvement will inevitably and inexorably follow.

THE COST OF QUALITY

Increased competition, deregulation, asset quality problems, noninterest expense growth, and merger activity have caused myriad problems for banks. The most serious of these problems include profit shrinkage, loss of market share, reduced growth, and depressed stock prices. Since 1980, the banker's world has changed dramatically, primarily because of deregulation, which has caused serious turmoil in the entire financial services industry. Banks are losing ground to foreign competition, noninterest expense continues to grow, and the stock prices reflect industry problems. All of these issues are, at bottom, related to the cost of quality.

"Cost of quality" is a phrase that is tossed around quite a bit. There are two costs of quality, the "good" kind and the "bad" kind. The bad kind is the cost of doing things wrong and redoing them, of doing things that don't need to be done, and of inspection and correction of defects. Juran identifies "bad" costs as "those costs that would disappear if products and processes were perfect."[1] Poor quality costs hard dollars in time, materials, and energy, and soft dollars in productivity, morale, and reputation. Banks must begin to think about what they do in terms of the functions and activities in their processes that are undertaken to ensure quality services are delivered.

The good cost of quality is prevention, or the amount that is

Table 4.1   Cost of Quality Activities

Attending Meetings
Preparing for Meetings
Complaint Handling
Report Preparation
Meeting Management
Reviewing Work
Conducting Meetings
Documentation
Adjustments
Verifying
Forms Completion
Quality Assurance
Inspection
Idle Time
Compliance
Legislative Review
Audit
Forms Management
Chargebacks
Regulatory Reporting
Data Recovery
Holdovers
Compliance
Tracing Work
System Recovery

spent to make sure that services delivered meet or exceed the customer's expectations, for the value being perceived. The price of prevention is what is necessary to spend to make sure that things come out right including training and education, planning, communicating, designing processes, and other quality actions. The ratio of prevention to inspection/correction can be used to track whether the company is improving and as a basis for finding out where the most important improvement opportunities are. Table 4.1 is a partial list of typical banking activities that contribute to the cost of quality.

The cost of quality appears on the balance sheet and on both sides of the income statement. It is not simply an expense problem. It is important to understand that the cost of quality is evident in every aspect of the bank's activities and is an asset, liability, fee income, and expense opportunity. There are many estimates of the cost of quality, usually given as a percentage of some other number such as sales, operating costs, or noninterest expense. Listed below are some of the various estimates arrived at by different sources:

30 percent of sales (Juran)

5 to 10 percent of sales, 40 percent of operating expense (Crosby)

17 percent of manufacturing costs (Deming)

15 to 20 percent of operating expenses (Crestar Bank)

30 percent of manufacturing costs (IBM)

20 percent of sales (Baldrige Award application)

20 to 25 percent of operating budget (Italian Bank Marketing Association)

25 percent of noninterest expense (BancOne Corporation)

30 percent of noninterest expense (J. D. Carreker, Inc.; Ernst & Young; McKinsey & Co., Inc.; First Manhattan Consulting Group)

There may not be specific agreement on the exact percentage of noninterest expense that makes up the cost of quality, or the best way to measure it, but it is agreed that it is a material amount. Philip Crosby goes on to say that when calculating the cost of quality, only about one-sixth of it is easily calculated while five-sixths is usually missed.[2] He also points out that more than 25 percent of nonmanufacturing work is routinely done over before it is correct. By any estimate, the cost of quality is a huge number. Due to the years when cost and price were determined by the government, activities proliferated that are not needed and quality has been confused with productivity.

Calculating the Cost of Quality

When estimating the cost of quality for an individual bank one should try to use the 30 percent of noninterest expense figure. However, eliminating the entire cost of quality may not be practical, so to obtain a realistic improvement target, a 15 percent reduction is used. After tax affecting that amount (additional tax must be paid on net income before taxes), the resulting number is added to the income and before- and after-QVE comparisons of ROA and ROE are made:

1991 Noninterest Expense	$285 Million
Cost of Quality	15%
Total Improvement Opportunity	$42.8 Million
1 - Tax Rate	65%
Total Benefit	$27.8 Million

	Before QVE	Estimated After QVE
ROA	1.05%	1.38%
ROE	16.10%	21.22%

Eliminating the cost of quality will increase these critical ratios and create sustainable advantage based on quality services and commitment to the customer. What does this mean? If money is spent to fix, correct, and redo things, it is spent needlessly. If money is spent needlessly, the cost to deliver services is higher than necessary. If the cost is higher than necessary, it can be reduced, providing pricing flexibility and increased margins. By reducing the amount of wasted effort, rework, and things that do not have to be done, unit costs are reduced, thereby increasing the contribution of each transaction.

Closing the Back Door

The "back door" refers to the one that opens and shuts when a customer leaves the bank for good. The economic impact of customer account turnover is created by the 35 and 45 percent of customer accounts that are closed are because of poor service. As an example, the weighted average rate of all accounts is 5.3 percent; the federal funds rate is currently around 9 percent. Assuming that account balances are replaced with federal funds, the replacement cost of those accounts is 3.7 percent. The following example calculates exactly what the dollar cost of poor quality is:

Total Account Turnover	20%
Percentage due to Poor Service	40%
Total Turnover due to Poor Service	8%
Total Deposits	$4.7 Billion
Deposits Withdrawn due to Poor Service	$375.0 Million
Replacement Cost	$13.9 Million

Calculate the cost of the back door using deposit base and turnover rate. Then try to factor in how many weeks or months the staff must work just to catch up to the previous year due to account closures. Add in the cost in morale problems and employee turnover. Quantifying those costs is extremely difficult; that doesn't mean they're not real.

Consider the asset side of the equation. A typical weighted rate of asset interest rates might be around 12.5 percent. Applying an 8 percent turnover rate could equate to a lost margin of $7.0 million:

Total Loans	$2.6 Billion
Loans Lost due to Poor Service	$204.0 Million
Lost Spread (12.5%–9%)	3.5%
Lost Margin	$7.0 Million

To the $7.0 million in lost margin must be added the loan fees that are also lost. Total fee income for a bank of this size and composition could be around $120.0 million. Therefore, fee income from the lost accounts could be as much as $9.6 million. With the back door open, the bank loses potential revenue of $30.5 million![3] Again, calculate the effect on lenders as they find themselves running just to stay in place. Stopping just 25 percent of them from closing would add 10 percent to the annual net income of this bank. The bottom line is that not only does it cost the bank unnecessarily to correct mistakes, handle customer complaints, re-engineer systems, and reprocess statements, but it is also very expensive when the customer finally decides that enough is enough and actually leaves.

Cost Drivers

The budget line items that comprise the cost of quality—compensation, supplies, equipment, marketing/advertising, and so on—are fairly obvious, if difficult to quantify. Several activities represent the cost of quality. On top of that, there are associated costs in lost fee income, funds replacement, and margin spread. What is harder to see is what actually drives the behavior that results in unnecessary expenditures on these items, those structural causes of the costs of an activity. These underlying causes are called "cost drivers."

Cost drivers are the psychological, behavioral, maybe subconscious reasons that expenses are incurred. Regardless of the effort undertaken to improve quality, it will fail if the cost drivers are not explicitly understood and eliminated.

Cost drivers are largely overlooked. Ignoring cost drivers is the fundamental, fatal mistake that most companies make when attempting to implement quality programs and especially reduction exercises. Without examining root causes and dealing with them, nothing really changes. Cost drivers are largely organizational and cultural in nature. It's not that people don't want to produce high-quality products and services. On the contrary, many organizations' cultures are dysfunctional for the very reason that they tend to subvert people's natural inclination to take pride in their work.

Negative cost drivers hurt an organization in two ways: through actual expenditures that are unnecessary and through lost opportunities. The biggest driver of the cost of quality is fear. The opportunity cost associated with fear is enormous: problems not surfaced; questions not asked; ideas not expressed; challenges not made; rules not broken; risks not taken. The actual costs are high, too. It is largely fear that leads to most corporate politicking, empire-building, turf-protecting, and "CYA" behavior. Why do people go to so many meetings, write so many memos, require so many signatures? Fear of loss, of failure, of being left out or outmaneuvered. There is lots and lots of fear in most banks.

Fear tends to breed other demotivators, such as mistrust and excessive control. These are largely responsible for much of the inspection and review work that is done. Rather than designing processes that eliminate special causes and narrow normal variation to an acceptable range, then trusting the process and the processor, most departments design complicated review procedures. Most managers consider "review of work" to be a standard management activity, but need it be? "Training" and "continuous improvement" would be better uses of management time.

Another organizational driver is internal competition. Many companies foster some degree of internal competition in the name of "intrapreneurship" or to motivate through pride and the desire to be a winner. A little of this goes a long way, and the negative consequences may outweigh the positive ones. Certainly it is not a good way to foster communication, either interdepartmentally or interfunctionally. When information is power and the powerful win, why share it?

Yet another driver is demotivators such as exclusive perquisites that divide employees into haves and have-nots. "Perks" such as paid parking spaces, cars and car phones, club memberships, travel services, and other executive benefits that are given to those who financially need them least foster enormous amounts of resentment that inevitably carries into the workplace.

Cost drivers cause expenditures in all three areas of quality: prevention, inspection, and correction. It has been shown that the same problem costs more to fix the closer it gets to the customer. Take this example related by Hiroshi Hamada, president of Ricoh.[4] After shipping and installing a number of new copiers, a production defect was found in the entire line. All existing copiers, including those already installed, had to be re-engineered to fix the problem. Ricoh estimated the cost of that error at each possible detection and prevention point:

Design phase	$35
Before procurement	177
Before production	368
Before shipment	17,000
Actual cost	$590,000

The cost to fix the problem was nearly *17,000* times greater than it would have been to prevent it in the first place! Lest you think this couldn't happen at a bank, consider this example. A New York savings bank received its passbook savings statements from an external supplier. Unknown to the bank, the supplier had "missiled in a patch" (computerese for implementing a software fix) which didn't work, and the interest calculations on the statements were wrong. The supplier's solution? Send them out anyway! Although other bank customers of this supplier had—incredibly—followed this advice, this bank ignored it and proceeded to fix the problem on its own. One of the key managers[5] in this process decided to use this example in his QVE Dialogue homework to calculate the cost of quality and made the following estimate:

MIS/DP staff	$12,000
Other staff	7,350
Extra reports' statements	540
Printer breakdown	1,000
Lost opportunity/productivity	~20,000
Subtotal	$40,890

His calculation didn't even include the lost productivity of indirectly involved employees who were unable to use the system for the three days it was down, the catchup time after problem resolution, the damage to the bank's image of reliability, wear and tear on the system, and the potential security risk. Even so, he considered that $41,000 was quite a lot to spend on someone else's mistake. But it was even worse than that. As he was working on this calculation, the marketing director happened by and together they worked out this additional expense to the bank:

Customers affected	4,500
Customers angry enough to tell others	10%
Number of people told (450 × 12)	5,400
Average cost to open new account	$75
Assume 50 percent extra effort to convince the 5,400	112.50
Potential customer turnover cost	$607,500
Grand Total	$648,390

The total for a problem that lasted three days was, as one executive noted, about the size of their marketing budget for one year. Obviously, prevention is the most cost effective "fix" of all.

ORGANIZING FOR QUALITY

When organizing for quality, three levels of organization have to be addressed: the organization structure of the company; the infrastructure of the initial quality program; and the ongoing quality structure. They're not entirely separate, but they are distinct.

Organization Structure

The phrase "lean and mean" does not immediately spring to mind when considering banks. The salient features of banks' organization has tended more toward the "fat and benevolent," at least until very recently. Many might call them "fat and mean." Even after rounds of layoffs and hiring freezes, most banks do not have optimal organization structures. They tend to be hierarchical, vertically oriented, and authoritarian. They are usually highly regulated internally and externally, with a tightly controlled distribution system and a centralized administration. They have *lots* of layers of management. The study conducted by NABCA showed that the average number of levels between the chief executive officer and the teller was six. The average for banks with assets greater than $10 billion was eight, and Security Pacific reported 15. Bureaucracy is formalized through the use of corporate titles—thousands of them.

It will strike nearly everyone reading this that this type of structure is out of synch with the current thinking in organizing, particularly contrasted to small startup companies and fast track industries such as information technology. It is generally recognized that cumbersome management structures and entrenched bureaucracy are inflexible, expensive, stifling, resistant, and slow to change.

QVE Infrastructure

The structure of Quality Value Engineering is based on quality and customer satisfaction, not on chain of command. The essence of QVE is the Value Creation Teams. Supporting them in numerous essential ways are the Value Added Teams. And cheering them on and providing resources is the Quality Council. Peripheral to the process are the Value Creation

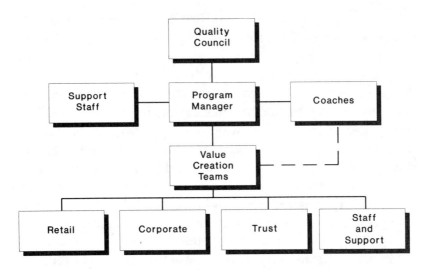

Figure 4.1. Quality Value Engineering Organization Chart

Coaches. (The organization chart in Figure 4.1 diagrams the QVE structure.)

The Value Creation Teams are comprised of 6 to 12 first- and second-level managers. Why managers, not workers? Remember what the quality gurus say: The workers are not the problem. Managers own and control the problem; they have to find the solutions. Furthermore, it is necessary to have their commitment to the process of continuous improvement. What better way than to make them responsible for establishing the culture of improving? These particular managers will be running the company someday. They need to have the spirit and techniques for continuous improvement. (Later, of course, it would be fine to have workers participate in the Value Creation Teams.)

The VCTs are interfunctional and consist of the users and providers of whatever service or product is being examined. They are essentially autonomous, although they report informally to the council, and on a dotted-line basis to the Value Creation Coaches. The leadership of the teams can be derived in several ways. The best way is to rotate the leadership responsibilities. This has several benefits. One is that no one person is stuck with the administrivia that comes along with leadership. The VCT process is demanding enough without burdening a single person with extra activities. Another is that full participation is ensured. But the most important benefit is that it emphasizes the egalitarian nature of the process, and helps ensure that the old hierarchical chains of command don't creep back. There are other ways of determining the leadership role, however. It may be assigned, based on natural abilities or, conversely, the need for an individual to develop those abilities. It may be volunteered for, or the leader may be elected. Using co-leaders is another possibility. Every company, indeed, every team, will want to determine the way that's best for itself.

Working closely with the Value Creation Teams are the Value Added Teams, so called because they provide additional brainstorming, problem-solving, process-unraveling power to the process. Since the VCT members are managers and supervisors, they will have workers reporting to them who can act in this capacity, and so the individual member's work unit will become the Value Added Team. Obviously, these teams will be functionally homogeneous, and therefore somewhat analogous to Quality Circles. There are alternative ways of forming VATs. For instance, members of the council may be chosen to work on the teams; VCT members from very small departments may choose to involve the entire department, including the department manager; or a branch representative may want to include representatives from other branches rather than using employees from the same branch. VCT members should be free to choose VAT members of their choice.

The VATs are full participants in the QVE process, and their role is merely different from, not subordinate to, the VCTs. VCT members act as facilitators, not managers, for the VATs. They must divorce the VAT role from the everyday role as managers; they will probably learn a new style of managing in the process. VCT members are expected to share knowledge, materials, and homework assignments from the Dialogues (discussed in Chapter 7), and will be critical in the process dissection and re-engineering phase.

The Quality Council is the corporate cheerleader. It consists of the senior managers of the organization, possibly including the president and/or chief executive officer. In addition to leading the quality effort, supporting the teams, and demonstrably committing to quality in every way, it oversees the entire quality process and makes policy decisions that ratify the quality initiatives undertaken, to make them part of the culture and of the way business is done at their bank.

The Value Creation Coaches are process facilitators, and they may be either internal or external, or both. If the program starts with external coaches, there should be a mechanism in place for converting to internal coaches within two to five years (depending on the size of the organization). These need not be formal, staff facilitators; in fact, it is preferable to train willing and able employees to take the role in addition to their regular duties. To a large extent this will occur naturally in the QVE process. As teams are formed and disbanded and the experienced members go back into the organization, they can be utilized as coaches with just a little special training in group dynamics and team-building techniques.

The coaches are on the same organizational level as the value creation teams and report directly to the council, although there is a faint dotted line between the coaches and the teams. The relationship is similar to that between sports teams and their coaches, in that coaches provide technical assistance in learning and using the value creation process, they facilitate team-building, they give pep talks when needed, and they help identify and overcome barriers to team success.

Figures 4.2–4.4 show the overall structure of the QVE program. Its structural characteristics are a marked contrast to those of most banks. The most striking feature is its orientation to the horizontal, rather than the vertical. It attempts to be supremely democratic and participative. Everyone is involved, in one way or another. The decision-making is decentralized and distributed throughout all levels of the organization. Corporate titles are eliminated and only functional titles are used, if indeed any are used at all. There is no false hierarchy, no artificial

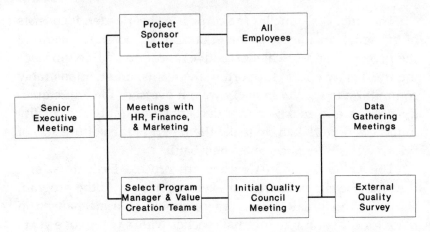

Figure 4.2. Quality Value Engineering Process Methodology

barriers to communication, no authority based merely on position. In many ways, QVE turns the organization chart upside down: customers (internal and external) are on the top calling the shots; the front line is gathering information and disseminating it "down" the ranks; the policy-setters incorporate the information into their strategic planning process and coordinate the implementation of customer satisfaction through policy creation.

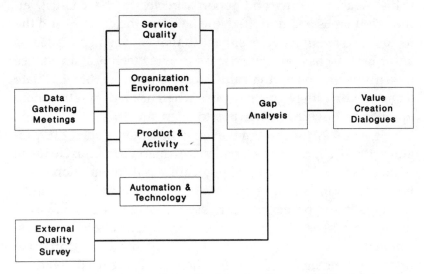

Figure 4.3. Quality Value Engineering Process Methodology

Figure 4.4. Quality Value Engineering Process Methodology

The program structure requires greater autonomy of workers and lower level supervisors, because it builds in the direct communication of information from customers to them, the front line, and therefore it is necessary for them to be able to respond appropriately and, especially, quickly. In fact, there are few actual "managers" in the QVE process. Someone has to manage the process, of course, but it is generally assumed that people can manage themselves. What managing there is takes a different form: Managers act to supply resources and coordinate efforts, rather than to assign and inspect tasks. It is the team members who decide what needs to be done, make or take assignments, and determine whether the results are satisfactory. This is a radical change.

Effect of Quality on Organization

Inevitably, this style of organization is going to spill into the old macro-organization. The old organization is going to start to feel heavy, plodding, restrictive. Change will occur. In some banks it will happen slowly, as Value Creation and Value Added Teams disband and their members rejoin the organization at large. They will subtly alter their own way of working with their employees, supervisors, and colleagues, and as a critical mass of employees is reached that has been through the QVE process, the culture will have been won over to the quality approach and the organization structure will be pulled along with it. Other banks will recognize almost immediately that their style of organization is no longer compatible with their new goals, and will seek to change the organization as part of their quality objectives. In fact, organization change is built into the QVE process, although the decision to implement always resides with the bank undertaking the process.

The kinds of changes that can and will occur are too numerous to list completely and are largely specific to a given bank (its former structure and style, its employees, its quality goals). But some of the changes that will be experienced by nearly every bank include the following:

- *Eliminating excess layers.* It seems as though everyone has done this already and yet there is still much bureaucracy built into banking organizations. Banks need to keep whacking away at it at all levels for two good reasons: They can't afford it, and they won't be able to fill it up when the baby bust hits. Wholesale layoffs of qualified, performing employees need not be implemented. "Resource redeployment" with job loss a last resort is a better strategy for banks that are in trouble.

- *Worker empowerment.* This is a buzzword but it refers to the process of giving greater autonomy and decision-making authority to all workers. Along with this is the concept of "self-control" that Juran talks about, which really means exercising individual responsibility. For managers, it means letting go—of information, problems, and sole proprietorship of "the buck."

- *Alternative models of organization.* There are many models out there already and endless possibilities exist. Some of the current alternatives include self-managed work teams, the upside down pyramid, hub-and-spoke organizations, and matrix management. These alternatives result in new roles for managers that are less technical and authoritarian and more service-minded. In fact, managers could become another type of worker, valued for their facilitating, resource management skills rather than their decision-making and leadership, since those skills will be assumed by or at least shared with the workers.

- *A discipleship of equals.* Every organization needs some kind of leader, and not every bank is going to be lucky enough to have a charismatic one, but the relationship between the leader and the rest of the bank can still be considered a "discipleship" if the leader truly values and is valued by the employees. Moreover, the leader needn't "play God" to make this relationship work; in fact, letting everyone be equal may be the best way to inspire loyalty and admiration.

- *Abandoning corporate titles.* Corporate titles reflect an insidious, built-in hierarchy that hampers flexibility and communication. They are virtually meaningless to outsiders and destructive to insiders. One bank, Royal Trust in Toronto, Canada, has made the leap to abandon these titles; two years later they are thrilled with the results. According to Bonnie Cornell, the public relations and communications director who was largely responsible for implementing the program, abandoning their officer titles for "partner" titles has truly changed the way they think about and relate to each other—all for the better. More banks should try it.

STRUCTURING THE ONGOING QUALITY PROGRAM

The QVE process is one that will galvanize the entire bank, and everyone will be involved at one time or another. At some point, however, an ongoing program of continuous quality improvement and customer service should be established. There are a number of issues that will determine the form a quality program takes.

First of all, there is the question of whose responsibility it will be. In other words, should responsibility for quality belong to everyone, both singly and as a group? If so, then there are matters to decide such as how to motivate such behavior and measure individual results. Many banks have solved this problem by doing explicit quality planning, as discussed in Chapter 3. Part of the quality plan incorporates quality goals into management objectives, along with financial, productivity, and other objectives. Quality can also be part of the performance criteria for workers and managers, as it is at First Tennessee Bank. Another alternative is to maintain the Value Creation Teams on either a continuous basis—it is difficult to imagine running out of problems—or to use them on an ad hoc, as needed basis. In either case, an appropriate reward system, such as gainsharing, should be put in place.

The argument against the "it's everyone's responsibility" approach is that things that are everyone's responsibility tend to become no one's responsibility. Again, the Value Creation Teams can be useful in ensuring that at one time or another everyone becomes involved, but at any given time a discrete number of individuals are assuming that responsibility. Also, the ultimate responsibility for quality always resides with the chief executive officer, who by now will have a keen desire and interest in maintaining the gains made through the quality strategy.

Another aspect of "everyone's responsibility" is the need for continuing quality education for all employees. Employees cannot be expected to stay at the forefront of the rapidly developing quality field in addition to performing their jobs and staying current in those technical developments. Therefore, classes in new techniques, seminars on recent innovations, and refresher courses in old methodologies will be required. This should consist of training by and for employees, as well as periodic updating by external quality experts. (This idea of continuing quality education will be covered in more detail in Chapter 6.)

The alternative to making quality everyone's responsibility is to form a quality department, headed by a chief quality officer. Needless to say, this CQO will be equal in rank and authority to the chief financial officer, chief administrative officer, chief operations officer, and other senior executives. There are advantages and disadvantages to this approach, too, of course. The primary advantage is that there are experts in-house who can keep abreast of the quality field and make the benefits of them available to the entire organization. There is an umbrella for the various quality initiatives taking place throughout the organization, which gives a measure of coordination and consistency and reduces the amount of wheel reinvention taking place. The disadvantage is that if there is a quality department, everyone else may abdicate personal responsibility for the effort and finger-pointing will begin.

If a quality department is the desired form of an ongoing quality program, several issues must be resolved satisfactorily:

- What is the mission of the department? To advise, inform, teach? To provide expertise and resources? To be proactive or respond to requests for assistance?
- What are the goals and objectives? (These will reflect the mission, of course.)
- How will it be measured? How can it take credit or assume blame for other departments' quality results?
- What expertise must reside in-house? What can be contracted out? Should the quality staff be centralized or decentralized? If centralized, will the department managers consider them to be staff interference? If decentralized, what will the coordinating mechanism be?

An obvious solution is to combine elements from both approaches. The Quality Council might function as sort of a higher level Value Creation Team. It would convene not only to solve specific quality problems but to deliberate on broader quality issues, such as when to offer additional training and what kinds; how to motivate and measure quality performance; determining what staff would be cost-effective in-house; and other quality policy and strategy issues. It might also be convened to design and manage, possibly to review, the annual quality planning process. And the same members would not comprise the team each time. A succession plan should be devised to keep interest fresh and provide broader participation. Retiring council members could pick their own successors. As with most things in QVE, however, this is not the only option; each bank should examine the alternatives and pick the one that seems right.

QUALITY CUSTOMER SERVICE

While banks have to go beyond customer service and into total quality, satisfying the customer through a combination of product and service excellence must be the goal of a total quality program. And it's clear that banks are not where they want to be. Table 4.2 reproduces a chart that appeared in the *Wall Street Journal*, rating the service level of various industries, including banks. Nearly 80 percent of the respondents said that bank service is getting worse or staying about the same; only 17 percent thought it was getting better. Only the automobile industry was rated lower. Banks thus have a major opportunity to differentiate through customer service.

Why are banks rated so low? One reason has to do with

Table 4.2 Service Providers? "How Would You Rate the Overall Level of Service These Industries Provide Customers?"

Respondents	Getting Better	Getting Worse	Staying about the Same	Not Sure
Supermarkets	31	18	50	1
Automobiles	24	37	31	8
Restaurants	22	19	56	4
Department Stores	20	29	48	3
Hotels	20	16	45	19
BANKS	17	29	50	4

The Wall Street Journal/NBC News Poll, November 12, 1990

their organization structure, already cited as an opportunity for change. Branch employees tend to be very compartmentalized in their functions; it is not uncommon to be shuffled from one line to the next or over to another area of the lobby in order to handle several different transactions. Efficient? Yes, but for whom? Not the customer. The authors of *Service America!* talk about the struggle banks had to get people to use ATMs, and of the strategies that were employed by banks to get customers to use a service that they had no need for and didn't want. That was back in 1984 and banks had the last laugh, because the preference has strongly swung the other way. But the banks were motivated by lower transaction costs, not customer need. Is that service?

WAR STORIES

Some banks are better than others, of course, but almost everyone can relate a war story. As Tom Peters says, "Let doubters reflect on their own treatment as customers. . . . Have them relate stories from friends and bank customers concerning service quality at financial institutions. Horror stories surface quickly." Some of the worst stories are from customers who are themselves bankers. Richard Detoy, a vice president at Security Pacific National Bank, still seethes when he recalls the two-and-a-half hours he waited to complete a relatively simple CD transaction for his son. Lance Weaver, a senior executive vice president for MBNA America, was visibly worked up by the time he finished his horror story of trying to rent a safe deposit box at a bank in the town he had just moved to. "They said they had no more available," he related. "They said it like they might never have any, and didn't care if they didn't!" As a banker, he could see what the implications of this attitude were for the bank: For the lack of a safe deposit box, it was going to lose checking and savings accounts, college accounts, IRAs, CDs, credit cards, and any other financial transaction he might make.

One of the authors went to a local branch of a bank in order to change her daughter's account from a trustee account to a CUGMA. Three times the assistant vice president she spoke with told her why it couldn't be done, and insisted that she go to the headquarters branch herself to have the change made. Needless to say, after making the inconvenient trip to downtown Los Angeles to do so, it was technically easy simply to close the account and open another at a different bank—and it was emotionally impossible to do anything else.

Sal Serrantino, president of California Research Corporation, tells the story of the bank he walked into at Christmastime. That's a very busy time of year for banks, but the teller lines were fairly short—except at one teller window. "This must be world's slowest teller," Sal thought to himself. But on closer look, he realized that the customers in the line were holding Christmas presents, and the teller had behind her stacks of Christmas presents. He moved closer to watch her work, and immediately revised his assessment. Far from being slow, she was extremely efficient. Yet she always had a friendly, personal word for each of her customers. And "her" customers they surely were, for they endured a long line just to wish her a merry Christmas and give her a present for the service she must give the whole year round.

SERVICE STRATEGY

Everyone has their favorite bank story, good or bad, but the fact is that banking's reputation for customer service is not what it should be. They know this, but many banks have not been able to put together a service strategy that will put them above the expectations of the customers and gain a competitive advantage from excellent customer service. It takes a lifetime to establish a customer relationship, and a bank can lose it in one minute with an arrogant customer service representative on the phone.

A service strategy is necessary for two main reasons: (1) to anticipate changes in the marketplace; and (2) to respond to a crisis. Anticipation should avert a lot of crises, but there will always be something that occurs that couldn't be predicted, and there should be a mechanism for dealing smoothly and quickly with that crisis. There are three key ingredients of a service strategy:

- *Market research:* Whether a bank does it or buys it, it has to know what customers want, what they expect, and how well they think the bank is providing it.
- *Business mission:* Service must be an explicit part of the bank's mission, and this mission must be reiterated and supported in the goals statement, the objectives, and the operating tactics.
- *Organization values:* These relate to the culture and cannot simply be dreamed up and slapped on a poster or silk-screened on coffee mugs. It all goes back to leadership and committing to quality.

The end goal of customer service is to attract customers who will become clients, in other words, who will stay with the bank a long time, bring all their business, and tell others about the bank. Loyal customers are special people. Understand that they come to a bank looking for a given level of service; they buy and are not sold, but they buy more than new customers; and they communicate their needs. Whereas a new customer will simply go elsewhere, a loyal customer will say what's wrong and how it can be fixed. That's invaluable.

It is as difficult, unfortunately, to define what good service is as it is to define quality. One definition characterizes customer service as conforming to requirements, with no defects, within acceptable limits of variation. Another definition is "staying ahead of the customer." That encompasses anticipation and adds, perhaps, the dimension of empathy—being sensitive to what the customer's needs are and what they may be. But it could also take customers where they don't necessarily want to go, as in the ATM example above.

Valarie Zeithaml et al., in *Delivering Quality Service*, identify five dimensions of service quality:

- *Reliability:* keeping the service promise
- *Responsiveness:* being prepared and willing to serve promptly and efficiently
- *Assurance:* competence and courtesy
- *Empathy:* individualized, caring attention
- *Tangibles:* the "seeable" part of the service offer (facilities, employee appearance, etc.)

These five dimensions point out the need for a little prework on the part of most banks. For instance, how can a bank keep a service promise it hasn't made? A lot of banks put "quality" and "service" into their advertising messages, yet not a single explicit promise is made, apart from some vague notion that a given bank is going to be better than its competitors in some unexplained way. How about promising to be prepared, willing, competent, and courteous? Banks spend lots of money on their lending officers to make sure those relationships go smoothly; but they are not willing to invest in the kinds of salaries and training to make their tellers, or customer service representatives, equally skilled. And they give mixed messages. Does individualized, caring attention really square with fast, efficient service *and* cross-selling? When push comes to shove, which is more important? Answering "all three" just isn't fair and it's not translatable into action.

There are significant gaps between the importance attached to the components of service quality management and the degree to which bankers are actually implementing the activities within their institutions. Nearly everyone feels that it is important, but they are having difficulty taking appropriate action.[6]

The fact is, customer service comes back to some fundamental premises: culture, commitment, and the need for total quality. Direct customer service, where a bank employee actually transacts business with a customer, is only the tip of the service quality iceberg. Figures 4.5 and 4.6 show why. These figures diagram the movement of a check from the time a customer writes it to the time it comes back in a statement. Every single transaction represents several chances for things to go right or wrong in the system. Every check passes through 30 different places in the system: 30 ways that the system can fail the customer; 30 chances to make or break that relationship. Multiply that times the number of checks passing through and factor in all the other transactions being made, not to mention all the other internal mechanisms that can affect individuals in the system, and it is evident that the probability for failure is very great and for success very small.

Of course, more often than not, the system works quite well. But even a 98 or 99 percent success rate means that a lot of customers are going to be unhappy with their month-end statements for one reason or another. Or with the way their loan was handled. Or with their service charges. And so on and on and on. The average customer with a complaint tells ten people; 13 percent tell as many as 20. Furthermore, 42 percent (some sources go as high as 68 percent) of customers who switch banks do so because of service problems.[7]

On the bright side, of the customers that actually complain about the service (96 percent do not), between 54 and 70 percent will return if the complaint is resolved satisfactorily, and they will tell an average of five people about their experience. Obviously it is important to resolve complaints, and banks have responded to this fairly well, instituting 24-hour customer service lines, paying customers for waiting in long teller lines, and other fixes. Very few have figured out how to prevent the problems in the first place, despite the obvious economic benefit to doing so. As pointed out earlier, the closer a problem gets to the customer the harder and more expensive it is to fix, maybe as much as 17,000 times more expensive than if it were caught just after it was made, not to mention not making it in

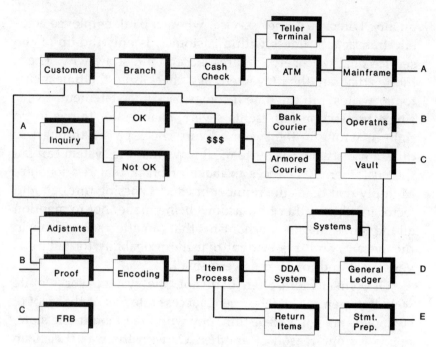

Figure 4.5. Check Cashing Process Flow

the first place. That's the cost side.

The revenue side is even more dramatic, in actual loss of market share due to the ripple effect of unhappy customers, and in the opportunity cost of not grabbing the bulk of unhappy customers from other banks and increasing market share. According to PIMS,[8] there is a direct relationship between market share and profitability, and quality has been shown to be a market share driver. Therefore, there is a positive correlation between quality and profitability.

Ensuring high-quality customer service means going back to the basics of banking, maybe even back, mentally, to the days of regulation when banks could afford to be courteous and gracious because they weren't dealing with the dog-eat-dog world of competition. There are five areas that must be addressed in order to achieve superior customer service: culture; management; leadership; employees; and organization

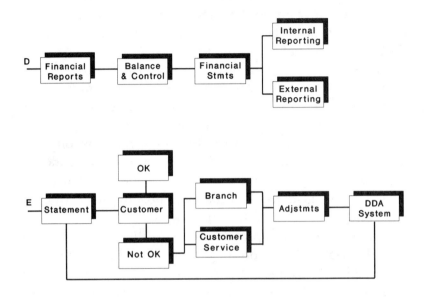

Figure 4.6. Check Cashing Process Flow

and work flow. It is easy to see why providing good service is not just the province of those front-line workers who actually meet the customer, and why reorienting the entire bank toward quality has to be the goal.

Instilling a quality service culture means focusing on the customer, identifying demands and designing products and services to meet them. It means training employees to want to serve, and providing them with efficient systems for delivering good service. Above all, it requires trusting the employees to do the right thing when new or unusual situations present themselves.

Once the culture has accepted quality service as its creed, the process must be managed. Managing may require using service quality management charts; there must be standards and measures that can be applied to individual and group performance, whether that group be a functional unit or a branch. Management will also ensure that implementation of innovations and improvement projects mirrors their importance; in other words, it will prioritize new ideas, not just according to the monetary benefit, but also, in line with the new culture, according to the benefit to the customer.

The senior leadership of the bank must be involved with service quality, as it must with any quality program or component. It must be willing to invest in a service infrastructure, such as updating systems and training. More important, it must be willing and able to focus on and plan for the long term, occasionally to the detriment of short-term results. Leadership must have the depth and breadth of vision to want to stay "ahead of the customer," in the most positive sense of caring about and responding to the customer's needs.

None of this will improve service quality if the right people are not on board. For too long banks have taken the people whom nobody could stand to work with and put them on customer service telephones, where they do incredible damage. Eventually, the culture will be such that those people will be uncomfortable and will want to leave; until then, they must be assigned positions as far away from customers as possible. For the rest, training will solve most of the problems. And obviously, the proper attitude toward service, customers, and quality will be one of the key features screened for in the recruiting process. First Tennessee Bank says that all their employees have the right attitude, because without it they simply cannot be effective in their jobs. MBNA America's hiring process includes interviews of *every qualified candidate for any position in the bank* by the executive managers. MBNA America, incidentally, has eight to nine candidates for every conceivable position, and virtually never advertises. Once the right people are on board, it becomes part of the leadership and management process to motivate the right behavior at every opportunity. This is done through rewards, incentives (and disincentives), peer pressure, and, above all, example.

The other side of the employee equation is how employees and their work are organized. The failure points in each organizational unit and each process must be identified and corrected. The best way to do this is with teamwork, for every process cuts across organizational and functional lines. Usually people don't even know where their work comes from or where it goes when it leaves their desk or their supervisor's desk. This kind of myopic suboptimization has to be eliminated if true effectiveness and efficiency are to be instituted. The identification and correction process should also include customers. Along the way it will be primarily internal customers until at the end some portion reaches the ultimate, external customer.

There is a common thread in each of the five quality service components: the customer. Demand side customer service is very different from most current forms of customer service, which are very much supply side. Supply side looks at processes first; it cares about cutting costs, downsizing, maximizing efficiency; it assumes it knows what the customer wants; it is organization-, operation-, and systems-driven.

Demand side customer service is customer-driven. It identifies internal and external customers. It determines their expectations of service and their perceptions of how well it is provided—and it determines these by asking customers. It moves to address the gaps between expectations and perceptions. And it reorganizes to provide only what the customer wants, at the level of quality wanted, and provides it right the first time, every time. Quality Value Engineering is demand side.

OVERVIEW OF QUALITY VALUE ENGINEERING METHODOLOGY

This chapter has introduced the QVE approach by discussing the three components of quality that must be included in a total quality program for financial institutions: the cost of quality; organizing for quality; and quality customer service. Addressing these three components will improve the profitability of the bank in substantial ways. This section of the chapter will outline how QVE incorporates the three components—and its highly desirable outcome—into a cohesive program that any bank can apply to itself. Chapters 5 through 7 will present the program in sufficient detail to be used as a "how to"; what follows is an overview of the steps involved.

It is important to understand that QVE is not actually a "program." It is not a series of steps taken to solve some identified problem. Of course, it could be used that way, but it would be a tremendous waste of an opportunity to do real good for the bank. QVE is emphatically not a quick fix. It is a focus and a technique, and it is very much open-ended. It is a methodology for instilling a customer and quality focus in the bank, and a tool to use in information-gathering and problem-solving. Quality Value Engineering is, in fact, a way of doing business.

There are ten discrete steps to QVE, with a great deal of overlap and concurrency in the implementation of it. The important thing to remember is that QVE is not a canned approach; it's a unique way of doing business. Each bank can incorporate its own quality initiatives, adding or deleting steps as appropriate, embellishing or simplifying. The ten steps are outlined in detail in the paragraphs below.

1. Organizing. Organizing refers to the process of setting up the quality program. It involves appointing the Quality Excellence Council, Value Creation Coaches, a project manager, and perhaps some staff. Farther along in the process Value Creation and Value Added Teams must be added, but this should wait until the products and services needing attention are identified so that the teams can be comprised of the appropriate service providers and users.

2. Prework. What kind of prework is necessary depends on where the bank is on the quality journey. Some of the areas that may need some assistance include commitment to quality by management, especially middle management; education of all employees through workshops or seminars; identification of internal and external customers; identification of the services and products to be surveyed, and matching these services and products to the appropriate customers; and customization of data collection tools to reflect the choice of products, services, and customers, and to address relevant cultural issues. (Both organizing and prework will be discussed in more detail in Chapter 5.)

3. *Data Collection.* There are three types of data collection that can be undertaken. One is surveys of external customers. Many banks have done this kind of survey and if information seems accurate and current, a bank may want to skip this step. (Pestering the customer is not considered a hallmark of good service, even when for a worthy cause.) Another data collection tool is the internal survey. All employees should participate. Data regarding the organization of people and work, culture, service expectations, and service perceptions should be collected. A third type of data collection is a quality self-assessment based on the criteria of the Baldrige examination.

4. *Analysis.* This is the only technical part of the process and will require some specialized software to do it really well. However, some of the software can be partially simulated. The data can be analyzed using readily available tools such as spreadsheet software to acquire a wealth of useful information. The result of the analysis is the identification of service gaps, and then prioritizing the areas to be addressed.

5. *Value Creation Teams.* There are three key pieces in this step. First, the Value Creation Teams and their Value Added Teams must be identified. (Value Added Teams do not have to be identified this early, but they may be. They should be well established by the second Dialogue.) Second, the method of leadership should be determined, and the team relationship developed.[9] Third, the Value Creation Dialogues must be undergone. (The Dialogues will have all of Chapter 7 devoted to them, because they are the heart of QVE.)

6. *Action Plans.* This plan is the outcome of the Value Creation and Value Added Teams' efforts over several weeks. It should be specific as to tasks, responsibilities, dates, expected costs and benefits, resources required, and completion criteria. It should be eminently actionable—containing small enough steps that results will be forthcoming in a reasonable period of

time, but broad enough that it will have some impact on the organization. The steps of the action plan must be synthesized to ensure that they are complementary and are real steps along the quality path. An action plan should, in sum, be a detailed roadmap for change.

7. Implementation. Implementation is highly dependent on the type of projects that are identified in the action plan, of course. Various tools can be used to make implementation easier.

8. Followup. Followup will depend on the projects undertaken. There are prototypes of forms useful in monitoring project results.

9. Rewards and Recognition. The form that rewards take is a highly cultural issue. Some institutions practice gainsharing and distribute a percentage of the project savings to the people who carried out the project. Others reject the whole idea of monetary rewards and use recognition and prestige as their reward systems. It doesn't appear to matter much which way a bank chooses to go, as long as it is fair and above all consistent throughout the organization. Monetary rewards are an excellent way to demonstrate true commitment to quality initiatives and to stimulate participation, especially after the first excitement of doing something new has worn off. Either way, recognition is essential to the success of quality improvement plans.

10. Continuing the Process. Quality is a journey. Quality Value Engineering is part of that journey, and therefore is long-term in nature, always open to innovations. Continuing to learn about developments in the field of quality improvement is integral to the QVE process. Perpetuating the teams, incorporating the newest findings and techniques, will ensure that quality improvement becomes an ingrained part of the bank's culture and all its processes.

NOTES

1. Joseph M. Juran, *Juran on Leadership for Quality: An Executive Handbook* (New York: Free Press, 1989), p. 199.

2. Philip Crosby, *Quality Is Free* (New York: McGraw-Hill, 1979), p. 28.

3. $13.9 million plus $7.0 million plus $9.6 million.

4. Story told at the Quality Forum VII, New York City, October 1, 1991.

5. Stephen Teti, assistant vice president, The Savings Bank of Utica, Utica, New York, October 1991.

6. "State of Service Quality Management, January, 1990," *Bank Marketing Association*. Survey of commercial banks conducted by the Bank Marketing Association, a trade group concerned with marketing and customer service issues (now merged with the American Banking Association).

7. Two other reasons why customers switch—hours (27%) and errors (22%)—are obviously part of the quality equation; the real number is probably closer to 93 percent.

8. Profit Impact of Marketing Strategies, database of marketing strategies—quality, productivity, advertising, and so on—correlated to profitability. Results first published in the 1970s.

9. There is an interesting phenomenon in group dynamics with special respect to small groups such as Value Creation Teams. The first reaction of each individual to the rest of the group is usually, "How did I end up with these turkeys?" After some time this is softened to, "Well, I guess they're not so bad." Eventually, a strong team identity is fostered that is extremely difficult to break. There are ways of hastening through the development phases and into the identification phase that are highly effective and should be applied if possible.

Chapter 5

Getting Organized

Here's the scene: You are a bank (or thrift, or trust, or credit union, etc.) of any size, doing business anywhere in the United States (or the world, for that matter). Your stockholders have expressed their dissatisfaction with their returns and stock values. Your managers are worried about the competition and pessimistic in their profit projections. Your employees seem uncommitted, at best, and your customer satisfaction surveys reflect it. You need help, and you're reading all over the place that quality is the way to go. Something called "Quality Value Engineering" sounds pretty interesting, and you think you'd like to give it a shot. What do you do?

QUALITY ASSESSMENT

The first thing is to run a self-diagnostic on the organization. The objective of the diagnostic is to assess exactly where you are in the quality journey, because where you are will determine what you need to do to get where you want to be. The specific objectives of the assessment are: (1) to find out what is working well, and to identify quality initiatives already in place; (2) to pinpoint trouble areas; (3) to solicit ideas about improvement opportunities; (4) to gauge the readiness of the culture to engage in a quality strategy; and (5) to design a customized program that will take all these factors into account. The assessment is necessary to tailor a Quality Value

Engineering program that will capitalize on *your* strengths, overcome *your* barriers and weaknesses, take advantage of known opportunities, and determine the kind and extent of prework to be undertaken prior to beginning an actual QVE study.

The emphasis, obviously, is on creating a custom-made program to suit your particular organizational needs. This book outlines the basics of QVE, what kinds of things to look for, ideas and solutions that are useful and effective. But you can't just read this and subsequent chapters and then overlay it onto your bank. To make it work, you have to do a fair amount of thinking and planning. And the first step is to get information on which to base your thoughts and plans. Hence, the assessment study.

The best way to find out what is going in the organization is to ask the people who work there. The kinds of things to find out are:

- the extent of management commitment, as evidenced by policies, processes in place, management style, performance criteria, and so on
- employee attitudes toward quality (Are they interested? Do they care? Is it important?)
- quality programs implemented, such as customer service training, SPC, quality circles
- the perceived strengths, weaknesses, and opportunities of the organization

Figure 5.1 provides a sample questionnaire. Questions should be open-ended, and although there has to be some standardization in order to make a good analysis, there should always be room and time for followup questions. This implies that questions are asked orally, in an interview, rather than through distributed surveys. Although interviews are more time-consuming and therefore somewhat limiting in terms of the number of people that can participate, the added flexibility of a "conversation" between interviewer and interviewee is

Employee Questionnaire

Organization: _____

Location: _____

Person Interviewed: _____

Functional Title: _____

Date: _____

1. Who are your customers?
2. Who are your suppliers?
3. What is your best product or service?
3a. If "quality" is not mentioned, ask the person to define "best."
4. Estimate the cost of quality in your area of responsibility (percentage basis—rework, redundancy, waste, etc.)?
4a. What are the major cost drivers?
5. What is the mission of your area of responsibility?
6. What is going well? What does your organization have going for it?
7. What is the biggest problem that keeps you from delivering your service?
8. What does your organization do best?
9. What is the mission of the bank?
10. Does anyone else in the bank do what your organization does? If so, who, where, and why?
11. If you had unlimited resources, what would you change about your organization and the bank?
12. What do your customers expect from you?
13. What do your customers think about the service you provide? How do you know that?
14. What could be done to improve the quality of your service?
15. Is quality important to the bank? Why or why not?

Figure 5.1. Quality Value Engineering Assessment Study

more important. Still, the more people that can be included, the more information that can be gathered. Try to talk to as many people as possible—up to 15 percent of the population in smaller banks, and at least 5 to 10 percent in larger banks.

The interview list has to be made up carefully. It is essential to include employees from every function, every major product, and all organizational levels. It is also desirable, at this point, to try to identify who actually have opinions and are assertive and reasonably articulate in expressing them. Of course, they must be assured that their remarks will be kept confidential, but there is little point in talking to people who have been with the bank for a short time, or who are unable to express their thoughts clearly. There will be ample opportunity for everyone to participate eventually.

It is an excellent idea to talk to a few customers, too. Arranged interviews are necessary for larger, corporate clients, but customers at branches are important as well. Customers can be approached in line. Start to ask questions. Soon other customers will begin listening and offering their opinions. Such a mini-focus group will provide a fabulous wealth of information.

The other group that must be included is the senior management team and the heads of the functional staff areas, especially human resources, marketing, and finance. Each of these will have a special role to play in the design and implementation of QVE, so it is crucial that their thoughts be incorporated into the general findings. Also, they will have the best idea of what quality-oriented policies are in place already.

When the information has been compiled and analyzed, there should be a fairly clear picture of where the organization is on its quality journey. It will be obvious whether or not the organization is ready to take the next steps, and what those next steps should be. The action to be decided on will be one of three: implement QVE immediately; do the necessary prework; forget about pursuing quality at this time. No bank should make the third decision, at least, none that wants to make the leap to competitive differentiation, increased market share, and superior profitability.

That leaves decisions one and two as acceptable alternatives. How will a bank know if it needs prework? There are two factors in particular to look for; if either is missing, do some upfront groundwork. The two essential pieces are *management commitment* and *employee attitudes*. All management, not just senior management, must be absolutely, positively committed to quality. And if employees aren't on board, forget the whole thing.

Management Commitment to Quality

Management commitment is the essential ingredient in the successful implementation of a quality program. As much as 85 percent of a company's problems are management-controllable; blaming and punishing the workers won't solve the problems, and implementing a "solution" that doesn't include management or that management doesn't believe in is doomed to failure. Deming attributes the failure of SPC in the 1940s, at one time so popular, to the lack of management commitment. Conversely, Juran says that "The critical element in Japan's success was top executive involvement."[1]

All the experts, from statisticians to behavioralists, agree on this point. Crosby makes it one of his four "legs" of a quality program, and deals with a company only if top management has signed on.[2] Deming also refuses to talk to any but the top leaders of companies, until he is assured that they are sufficiently committed. One of Juran's major contributions was the definition of management's roles and responsibilities in following a quality strategy. First Tennessee Bank will point to their management commitment as the key factor in their successful program. And Milliken, winner of the 1989 Baldrige for small business, said that they encountered only three problems when they began their quality journey: senior management, middle management, and lower management.[3]

How does a bank know if its managers are sufficiently committed? Look for visible demonstrations, not just lip service, that they are practicing quality management techniques such as participative management, facilitating and not just ordering, promoting and practicing teamwork. Find out what quality initiatives have been implemented and determine what the manager's role in them is on an ongoing basis. Make sure that the signals put out about quality are clear and unambiguous. If a bank is talking innovation but measuring productivity, teaching service but counting sales, or pushing quality until the next deadline or the end of the quarter, it's putting out a mixed message.

Quality should be explicitly included in the strategic business plan. Quality goals should be defined, assigned, committed to, measured, and tracked against performance. If quality is not in every manager's business plan, MBO, or commitment plan, it is probably not going to be done.

Finally, assess managers and organizational culture. Do they have the ability to let go, trust, and change? Are they die-hard authoritarians or can they really work with people? Does the organization reward risk and innovation? If not, it is a safe bet that the managers are not risk-takers and innovators. Are there people-oriented policies in place? It is difficult to implement quality strategies in a place that doesn't care much about people. Do managers believe that quality is a profit strategy? Do they believe it enough to give it a fair try?

If management commitment is less than it should be, there are remedial steps. First and foremost among these is education. Send managers to workshops that cover various aspects of quality: cost, organization, customer service, tools, the Baldrige Award. Let them read the section on "the cost of quality," and have them fill out the worksheet in their own areas. Let the workers be brought into the exercise; the resulting figures could convert them then and there. Get your managers to talk to managers in other banking and nonbanking companies who already have that commitment. Use a test site in the bank and see what the results are. Chances are they will want to see the same results in their own areas.

The only thing that prevents managers from committing to quality is their lack of knowledge and understanding that quality is, at bottom, a profit strategy. Once they understand how and why that is so, it is only a few steps farther to enthusiastic commitment. A couple of the other steps that may be required include team-building, participative management, and reward systems that recognize quality achievements. Some, of course, may require a personality overhaul that is well beyond the scope of this book and the ability of most companies. Those managers may find that they become "ineffective in their jobs."

Employee Attitudes

Clearly employee attitudes are going to reflect management commitment. But even if management commitment is present and genuine, employees may lag behind and show little enthusiasm. There are several plausible reasons for this. None of them have to do with the inability of workers to take pride in their work.

Employees are jaded. They have seen too many fads-of-the-month come and go. They're conditioned to respond just enough not to get into trouble, but not so much that anything actually changes. That makes it easier when that fad dies and the next one comes along. They are skeptical. They've heard the noise about quality but they know they're still being exhorted to work faster, do more with less, make up for laidoff colleagues, and sell, sell, sell. They are disenfranchised. They do all the work and management gets all the glory. Their input is neither solicited nor valued. Some may benefit from productivity incentives, but few get to participate in the ownership or profitability of the bank. They are ignorant, but this is not their fault. No one has taken the time to tell them how quality can affect their jobs, how it can let them be more creative, more involved, more effective, and, yes, more productive.

There are two solutions to the problem of employee attitudes: education and time. Educational workshops on quality will go a long way toward getting them on board, once they see what it will mean to them personally, how it will improve their work life. But only time will convince them that management is serious this time. Only by living through a missed processing deadline, a few quarters of reduced profits, a downward blip in market share—and still hearing the same quality messages that they got when the program started—will they begin to believe that quality is the strategy that their bank is truly following. Only then will the urge to do work that they can be proud of and to participate in a job and a company that they enjoy express itself enthusiastically.

GETTING STARTED

There are seven major tasks that must be accomplished preparatory to conducting QVE. This is necessary prework, the thinking and planning stage, which will enable the whole process to run smoothly and get the desired results without turning the entire organization upside down. The tasks are:

1. Structuring the program
2. Determining goals and objectives
3. Developing policies
4. Education and communication
5. Committing resources
6. Preparing tools
7. Scheduling

Structuring the Program

Three of the program's structural components must be identified up front: the Quality Excellence Council; the Value Creation Coaches; and the support staff. Generally, the executive management team will comprise the council, but it may be desirable to have other key managers or employees, possibly members of the board of directors and even customers and suppliers, sit on the council. The Quality Excellence Council will serve as the executive management of the QVE process. Its duties are to set policy, provide internal and external communication about the process, attend workshops that are given during the program, and visibly demonstrate commitment and participation. It is helpful to have one or more liaisons to interact directly with the teams, and a centerpost for administrative details. All members are responsible for advising and visibly supporting Value Creation Teams, smoothing rough areas in work schedules, addressing resource scarcity, and so on.

The Value Creation Coaches may be internal, external, or a combination of the two. If external consultants or facilitators are used, the project plan should include a clear method for transferring skills and information to some internal group, whether that be a staff area, experienced members of the teams, or the Quality Excellence Council. There should be a time, even if it can't be specified, when the external coach leaves and the company itself, through its internal coaches, assumes direction of the process.

Some support staff will be needed. They should report either to the council, the coaches, or both. This staff will be invaluable in coordinating and scheduling rooms and times for interviews, data collection, presentations, and the Dialogues. They can act as receiving and sending points for materials required for the Dialogues, and for typing and disseminating minutes and other important communication. There should be a central location for all materials—agendas, literature, minutes, memos—which may be used as a reference library for the team members and, indeed, any employee.

The other aspect of the program structure that should be settled immediately is whether QVE will be implemented company-wide right away, piloted at a test site, or brought in a department or function at a time. The choice that is made will depend largely on the size of the organization, the urgency of the need, and the organization culture. The advantage of doing it company-wide is that everyone gets to participate and there will be a much greater impact on the organization. Since many of the projects will narrow the focus anyway, and since so many processes are cross-functional, this is the best way to go if possible. There will be auxiliary benefits from this approach, such as identifying duplicated work, having more locations available for resource redeployment, and making various comparisons across the organization.

In a very large bank, however, it is probably preferable to implement QVE more slowly. Logistics alone are daunting in an organization with more than, say, 2,000 employees. There are additional advantages to using a test site or implementing QVE piecemeal, in that there is ample opportunity to customize the process further, to work out bugs, and to demonstrate results to the skeptics. This path may also be a deliberate method for gaining commitment from those who are not yet believers in the quality approach.

Determining Goals and Objectives

The second task of the Quality Council (after electing or appointing a program sponsor) is to formulate the goals and objectives of the program that speak to two questions: Why quality? Why now? It may want to develop a mission statement along the lines of the "vision statement" created by American Savings Bank in Irvine, California:

> American Savings Bank will be recognized by its customers, employees, and competition as synonymous with world class quality and integrity. This will be evident in the relationships we establish with our customers, the way we treat our employees, the performance of our balance sheet, the efficiency and productivity of our work units, and the consistency of our earnings.[4]

Or it may want to consider the approach taken by the Savings Bank of Utica in Utica, New York. Its Quality Excellence Council drafted a set of "Ten Commandments of Quality Service":

1. *Customer Expectations*
   Customer expectations shall always be met or exceeded.

2. *DIRFT*
   Do it right the first time (every time).
3. *DIRST*
   (Recognizing that an occasional mistake is part of the human experience), do it right the second time. Doing it right the second time includes correcting the mistake in such a way that the person who suffered the inconvenience of the first mistake is left with an overall positive feeling from the recovery process. In this way, DIRST is actually more important than DIRFT.
4. *Timeliness*
   Do it in a timely manner.
5. *The Collective "We"*
   There is no "we/they" or "I/mine"—only "we/us."
6. *Do unto Others . . .*
   Treat all customers (both external and internal) only as you would expect to be treated.
7. *Enhancing the "We"*
   Every customer contact (both external and internal) is an opportunity to improve (or to damage) the collective "we/us."
8. *Process focus*
   Focus on process; the results will take care of themselves.
9. *Fear of the Status Quo*
   Fear not change. Rather, fear the status quo. Do not fear failing. Rather, fear not trying.
10. *The Why Question*
    Quality is everyone's responsibility.
    Do not hesitate to ask "why" (as opposed to "how"). If no satisfactory answer is given, repeat it, again and again.

Along with the mission or vision statement, the council should identify expected outcomes of the program in terms of the entire organization as well as functions by organizational role and level. The outcomes should be quantified as much as possible. Appropriate measures and measuring tools would be very useful, although this may not be possible so early in the process. A time frame for the initial project should be established, bearing in mind that QVE is intended to become a business strategy, not a "project" in the sense that it ends when some predetermined goal is met. A comprehensive statement of purpose should be framed that can be communicated to the employees.

Developing Policies

The Quality Council will want to establish a number of general policies right away regarding the organization's official attitude toward quality in general and toward QVE specifically. The umbrella policy should be something along the lines that "Quality has priority over virtually everything else." A few things might take precedence over quality—such as a sudden health crisis of an employee or acts of God—but certainly the organization will no longer kowtow to anything so trivial as short-term results, supplier defects, or artificial deadlines.

Other general policies will be needed regarding the availability of human resources and the time commitment involved in carrying out the program. It will not do for a first-level supervisor who is a Value Creation Team member to have to work undue overtime in order to meet both job and team commitments. Other arrangements will need to be made and other resources made available.

One area of policy-setting that will be very important is that of human resources or personnel. The people in that area should be given free rein to develop creative policies regarding reward systems—a talent bank (human resource redeployment); displacement packages (as a last resort); promotions; and team participation, among others. It is best to implement a "no layoffs" policy if at all possible. (This policy is discussed further at the end of the chapter.)

TO: FELLOW EMPLOYEES
FROM: PRESIDENT
DATED: JUNE 6, 19XX
SUBJECT: SERVICE QUALITY ASSESSMENT

As you all know, over the past few years we have been working hard to improve the quality of the service we deliver to our customers and have made some major accomplishments.

Continuing to raise the quality level of our service is the only way we can make the bank even better, and we have begun a new process designed to do just that. Our purpose is to insure that each of us is doing the tasks and activities that our customers, both internal and external, want and at the quality level they require. As we begin the process, we need to determine exactly where we are on the quality journey, and to make that determination, I need your assistance.

We have invited Janet Gray and Tom Harvey of the firm of Value Concepts, Inc. to help us. The reason we have selected Janet and Tom is that they are not "efficiency experts" who will save the bank lots of money. Their role will be to serve as consultants to our "Process Engineering Project" and to help us organize to better meet the challenge of providing service which is perceived by the customer as top quality. Janet and Tom started Value Concepts to encourage financial institutions of our size to improve the quality of our services and are in the midst of writing a book . . . Starting on June 17, they will be with us for a few days to perform their Service Quality Assessment which consists of person-to-person interviews about the service we provide here.

In this Assessment, they will meet with a cross-section of about 50 of us to gather our input on a variety of subjects related to service quality. Their questions are not of the "Yes," "No," and "Sometimes" variety. Rather, they use discussion techniques since they are in search of how each of us does our job and views on our quality efforts, and want us to provide more information than a simple "yes" or "no." Those of you who are asked to participate should be able to spend about 45 minutes with Janet or Tom, and we would hope that you would want to do so.

Please be assured that there are no right or wrong answers. The purpose is to find out what we think about the way we service our

Figure 5.2. MEMORANDUM

customers. Your answers will be kept "Confidential," but they will be summarized for review and planning. It is our intent to use the combined results to further improve the quality of the service we provide. The goal is customer satisfaction. We will be sharing the results of this fact-finding effort, hopefully by the middle of July.

Janet and Tom have emphasized to us that the Assessment is a time for a free exchange of ideas, for you to tell them what quality means to you, and to offer some thoughts as to how you would make it better. They encourage us to be creative and innovative in the ways we approach our daily responsibilities.

As I mentioned at the beginning of this letter, service quality is our first and foremost obligation to our customers. We are excited about this opportunity, and it is important that we have your input. If you have any questions about the Assessment, please be sure to call me.

Thanks for your cooperation.

Figure 5.2. (*Continued*)

Education and Communication

Once the senior management has its ducks in order with respect to why it is pursuing a quality strategy and particularly why it is employing Quality Value Engineering, what it expects to achieve by doing this, and what policy guidelines are to be followed during the process, the rest of the employees should be told. Some may have been involved already, if the bank has performed an assessment study. In any case, a formal communication should be sent to all employees to let them know what will happen and, equally important, what will not, in terms of their jobs and their time commitment. Figure 5.2 is a memorandum that was actually used at a bank to announce the advent of the assessment study. A similar memo was distributed prior to the beginning of the Quality Value Engineering project. Notice in particular the collegial tone of the memo, the use of "us" not "you," the salutation to "Fellow Employees." This is a good time to introduce and qualify the facilitators, whether they be internal or external.

It is essential that communication be frequent, particularly at the beginning. As part of the orientation toward quality improvement, information must be broadly and regularly shared with employees at all levels. Assessment study results, survey findings, and team activities are all interesting and relevant to every employee, not just those directly affected by the project. Ultimately, remember, the goal is total participation.

Another important aspect to remember about communication is that it must be consistent; each new communication must reinforce not only what has been said before, but everything that the bank does must emphasize its commitment to quality. The public relations area might want to consider a complete package of media·communications that ties together advertising, shareholder relations, and other public and private messages.

Committing Resources

Obviously the most important resource to be concerned with is the human one—the employees. All of them must be involved and dedicated to the program, but their actual participation, at least initially, will vary depending on their organizational level and where they happen to work. Table 5.1 summarizes the roles and probable time commitments of various employees. All employees will participate in the data collection. Some first- and second-level managers will become members of Value Creation Teams, and therefore their direct reports will form Value Added Teams. Senior managers will be heavily involved in policy development, goal-setting, and general cheerleading. One senior manager will act as liaison and have a fairly heavy time commitment. Other managers will be asked to review the dictionary of activities and/or the survey questions. All managers will be asked to exercise patience and forebearance as their employees are occupied in various stages of the project. Some employees may have slightly increased workloads, due to the participation of other employees on the teams.

There will be special requirements of some of the staff. The

Table 5.1 Roles and Responsibilities

Senior Executives	Serve as Quality Council of the Project. Be available to set goals, prioritize issues for the Value Creation Teams, evaluate action plans. Generally sponsor and support the commitment to quality and the QVE program in particular.
Project Manager	Act as liaison between facilitators and the Quality Council. Provide insider historical and political contextual information. Assist Value Creation Teams in developing action plans and preparing presentations.
Senior Managers	Enable lower-level managers and employees to devote sufficient time to the Quality Value Engineering process. To assist them as requested.
First- and Second-Level Managers	Participate on Value Creation Teams. Attend ten six-hour meetings, complete homework assignments. Contribute creative ideas. Research and document ideas for implementation. Share responsibilities and results with Value Added Team.
Selected Workers	Participate on Value Added Teams as requested. Support supervisors in their work on Value Creation Teams.
All Employees	Offer candid opinions on organizational aspects surveyed. Keep an open mind about QVE, its goals and objectives. Participate fully in whatever capacity needed to make QVE successful.
Staff Assistant	Help with project logistics such as arranging the off-site meetings; scheduling data-gathering meetings; scheduling Value Creation Dialogues; arranging accommodations; serving as receiving/delivering point of contact; possibly light typing or copying
Process Engineer	Work in an advisory capacity with the Value Creation Teams in flowcharting the processes under study.
Financial Specialist	Work on financial measuring and monitoring systems and provide necessary financial data.
Systems Engineer	Advise the Value Creation Teams on the current state of technology and help determine where technological solutions to identified problems are appropriate and feasible.

human resources department, for instance, will be very involved in policy development in its areas, as mentioned above. They will spend a fair amount of time creating programs to cover incentives and other rewards; suggestion programs; the talent bank or similar concept; and displacement and severance, if necessary. They will also be involved in determining how best to include service quality standards in MBOs or whatever performance measurement system is already in place, or to develop new systems.

The marketing or public relations department will need to assist in identifying the customers to be surveyed and designing customer questionnaires. They will also help identify which services and products should be evaluated, based on some criterion of profitability, volume, strategic or competitive importance, or something else. They should spend considerable time establishing public relations campaign plans and tying these in closely with internal programs. They will also be invaluable in gathering and analyzing customer response data, since they are probably familiar with this type of information and can relate it to other, similar responses gathered previously.

The finance department will be especially useful in calculating the cost of quality—not an easy thing at all if it is true, as Crosby avers, that one-sixth is obvious and five-sixths is impossible to find. They can also help set reasonable financial objectives based on the cost of quality, and calculate the effects of these objectives on key management and shareholder measures such as ROE and ROA. Perhaps most important, they can develop a measurement system that is effective and workable based on their knowledge of the accounting and other financial systems in place.

Other resources besides human will have to be considered, of course. Money is chief among them. Is quality free? Initially, probably not. A brand new startup company has a shot at instilling quality for free in the way it organizes and trains the employees, in the systems it installs, and in the philosophy it espouses. Everyone else has to work with what they have, and that means investing some time and also some money. There will be expense associated with education, training, paying consultants to run the program, giving gifts for participating in data collection, rewards, recognition ceremonies, external communications, and various symbols that represent quality internally and externally. There will be additional expense in implementing the recommendations that are the outcome of the Value Creation Teams' efforts, for such things as retraining, hiring, systems solutions (hardware and software), machines, tools, consulting expense for followup work, industrial engineering or productivity analysis, and implementation assistance.

But remember: The expenses enumerated above are just a tiny drop in the bucket of the cost of quality. A quick and dirty estimate of the cost reveals that it's in the millions of dollars. Wouldn't that pay for a few coffee mugs or hours of consulting? Implementing a quality program has got to have the best ROI of any investment imaginable.

To make believers out of employees, customers, the board of directors, and shareholders means sharing information with them that certain departments have long considered their personal and private resource. Employees will have to learn to share with each other, managers will have to learn to share with workers. That doesn't mean that nothing is confidential, of course. But there can be no more withholding of critical information for purposes of gaining power, avoiding blame, wielding authority, or simple spite. The organization must "demystify" itself and share customer information, competitive data, process knowledge, goals, and destinations. People must be willing to communicate. Without this, QVE fails. There is not, and cannot be, quality.

Preparing Tools

There are five data collection tools that will be used, and each of them must be customized for the individual organization. The tools are:

- Dictionary of activities
- Organization environment questionnaire

- External customer quality service questionnaire
- Management survey
- Internal products/services survey

Dictionary of Activities

Part of the data that is gathered has to do with the activities that are performed regularly by employees. Since even employees who do the same job will describe it in different language, it is convenient to develop a dictionary of activities that will provide common terms and descriptions. That way employees can simply pick out the activities that are part of their jobs, rather than having to try to remember all the tasks that are performed and deciding which are the most important or representative. This will make data collection go more quickly and easily, and provide for comparability among jobs and between different functional areas.

A dictionary can easily be compiled by reviewing job descriptions, picking out the salient activities, and writing brief definitions for them. Some activities that are commonly performed but often are not included in job descriptions include: reviewing work, going to meetings, correcting work, and general management. Support activities such as these are taken for granted in organizations, but often contribute to poor quality. A sample page of a dictionary is shown in Figure 5.3. The dictionary of activities can be compiled by a project staff worker but should be reviewed at various levels throughout the organization for accuracy and completeness. Also, an effort should be made to use company-specific or department-specific terminology so that employees feel at home with the dictionary. A complete dictionary might contain between 350 and 600 activities and descriptions.

Organization Environment Questionnaire

There are various models to describe organizations, each made up of various numbers of components. QVE uses a model

242	ACCOUNTS RECEIVABLE	Posting billing to customer accounts; applying payments to customer accounts; managing accounts receivable systems.
162	ADDING MACHINE OPERATION	Operating noncomputer tabulating machines.
039	ADJUSTMENTS	Locating and correcting errors and preparing entries necessary to balance.
361	ADVERTISING	Design and preparation of advertising with promotional media. Includes working with agencies and media vendors.
362	ADVICES—DEPOSITS	Write letters notifying clients of deposit activities or results.
363	ADVICES—LENDING	Write letters notifying clients of lending activities or results.
330	ANALYZE CREDIT— CONSUMER	Analyzing the credit worthiness of applicants for consumer credit, and recommending a definitive course of action.
321	ANALYZE CREDIT— CORPORATE	Analyzing the creditworthiness of applicants for corporate credit and recommending a definite course of action.
323	ANALYZE CREDIT—FINL. INST./GOVERNMENT	Analyzing the creditworthiness of financial institution/government applicants for credit and recommending a definite course of action.
285	APPLICATION DEFINITION	Determining application feasibility; developing definitions and operating procedures for both new applications and application enhancements; reviewing available external pack-

Figure 5.3. Sample Dictionary Page

ages; defining business functions, processing requirements, controls, security and audit requirements of proposed applications.

286 APPLICATION CHANGE MANAGEMENT

Managing user requests for changes to existing or proposed computer applications; developing and maintaining standards and practices among user groups to coordinate those changes.

287 APPLICATION CONVERSION

Planning, coordinating and implementing conversion of application software.

288 APPLICATION DESIGN/ PLAN

Providing technical implementation plans and identifying the optimal environment for applications including hardware selection, data placement, data element/structure/relationship definition, backup/recovery recommendations, program specifications, and network recommendations.

Figure 5.3. (*Continued*)

that contains seven variables: mission, leadership, communication, human resources, systems, structure, and rewards.[5] Analyzing information about these variables will provide an exceptionally complete picture of the organization's culture, its patterns, and its physical composition. Questions should be designed to gauge not only *what is*, but what employees think about what is and what they think it should be. It is most convenient to use a "degree of agreement" approach and then to ask similar questions in different ways to pick up discrepancies and inconsistencies. Figure 5.4 shows one page of an organization environment questionnaire.

Organization Environment

Part I.	Strongly Disagree					Strongly Agree
1. My unit exists to serve its users.	1 2 3 4 5 6 7					
2. There is a lot of communication between different functional areas.	1 2 3 4 5 6 7					
3. I have or know where to get the information to allow me to do my job.	1 2 3 4 5 6 7					
4. My current skill level is adequate for the job.	1 2 3 4 5 6 7					
5. I am basically satisfied with my salary.	1 2 3 4 5 6 7					
6. Sometimes the employees are the last to know what's going on.	1 2 3 4 5 6 7					
7. My supervisor creates an atmosphere that is pleasant to work in.	1 2 3 4 5 6 7					
8. I know how my unit fits in with the rest of the bank.	1 2 3 4 5 6 7					
9. My work flow is logical and efficient.	1 2 3 4 5 6 7					
10. I have all the necessary tools to be effective in my job.	1 2 3 4 5 6 7					
11. I understand how my work fits into the whole process.	1 2 3 4 5 6 7					
12. The opportunities for advancement are good.	1 2 3 4 5 6 7					
13. There are enough people to do the necessary work.	1 2 3 4 5 6 7					
14. We spend a lot of time "fighting fires."	1 2 3 4 5 6 7					
15. My job priorities are clearly defined for me.	1 2 3 4 5 6 7					
16. The organization of my unit makes sense to me.	1 2 3 4 5 6 7					
17. I feel free to make suggestions about work improvements.	1 2 3 4 5 6 7					
18. The grapevine is usually the best source of information.	1 2 3 4 5 6 7					
19. I get personal satisfaction from my work and my job.	1 2 3 4 5 6 7					
20. The morale level seems to be high.	1 2 3 4 5 6 7					
21. My manager applies policies fairly and consistently.	1 2 3 4 5 6 7					
22. My work has a direct effect on the success of the unit.	1 2 3 4 5 6 7					
23. I am impressed with the quality of leadership here.	1 2 3 4 5 6 7					

Figure 5.4. Sample Organization Environment Questionnaire

External Customer Quality Service Questionnaire

The first step in designing this tool is to identify the products and services that are to be surveyed and then match them to customers to be surveyed. As mentioned above, the marketing department should be equipped to handle this. Naturally, it is important not to bias the sampling, so matching should either be random or with a great deal of thought given to distributing the questionnaire to as representative a population as possible.

The external customer questionnaire seeks to determine what quality features customers expect to find in various products and services, and also from the employees who provide them. It is usually best to provide some ideas of things they might expect, but also to leave some questions open-ended, especially toward the end of the questionnaire when their thinking has already been stimulated along quality lines. The second part of the questionnaire asks customers to match their perceptions of the bank to the expectations that they hold. Additionally, the questionnaire should try to gauge the strength of the demand for the product or service. Whether it is viewed as a luxury or a necessity will help determine the level of quality that must be associated with it, and possibly whether it should be offered at all.

Management Survey

Management is responsible for determining what customers want and need and translating it into products, services, and systems for delivering them. If their understanding is faulty, the whole structure is flawed. The management survey is designed to find out management's perception of customer demand and customer expectations, and of how well those requirements are being met. These are then matched against customer perceptions and expectations to see how closely they fit.

Internal Products/Services Survey

Every employee is a customer and supplier of internal products and services. This survey is, therefore, similar to the survey of external customers in determining the expectations and perceptions of quality levels associated with these products and services. The steps to designing this survey are as follows:

1. Identify the internal areas to be surveyed. Human resources is a good one because virtually everyone has some experience with it. Human resources can be surveyed as an entity or broken down into the various categories of services it provides such as employment, relations, and policy, or into specific products such as training courses, employee manuals, and benefits programs.

2. Match frequent users with services and products. Although nearly everyone uses human resources at one time or another, the same is not true for other internal services such as finance, legal, marketing, central purchasing, facilities, data-processing, and other support areas.

3. Gauge expectations and perceptions as in the external customer and management surveys.

4. Customize the data collection forms. This may be the trickiest part of the tool preparation phase. Because not everyone uses the same services to the same extent, the data collection forms will not be the same for each person. Forms will have to be sorted and organized in such a way that users are correctly matched with the products and services they are qualified to evaluate.

Tool preparation may be the most difficult part of preparing for a Quality Value Engineering study; as it is, it is not all that difficult. It is always worth it to take time up front developing the tools to use. As the saying goes, measure twice and cut once.

Scheduling

There will be a fair amount of logistical work for the project support staff in scheduling the various interviews, data collection meetings, and Dialogues.

External customer surveys should be developed and distributed as early as possible in order to have as many returned as possible. They should be a first priority in the project, and followup will be necessary to get a good return. Determine the distribution system(s) to be used (mail, telephone, branches, etc.).

All employees must be assigned to a data collection session. Try to schedule no more than 30 to 40 employees to a session; there will probably be questions, and it will be difficult to respond if there are too many people. Data collection should take no more than 45 minutes; scheduling meetings an hour apart should give sufficient time to any who are a little slower as well as giving a small break to the facilitators. Of course, there is no reason why someone who is taking longer should not simply continue to stay through the next session. Be sure makeup sessions are available for those who are absent for some reason.

Dialogues are the most difficult of all to schedule as they extend over a minimum of 20 weeks. Dialogues should be scheduled for at least six hours every two or three weeks. Considerable juggling of schedules will be necessary, but it should be emphasized to team members that this is their most important commitment for the next five months.

OTHER PROJECTS

Can and should a bank undertake other projects in conjunction with a Quality Value Engineering project, specifically productivity and cost-cutting projects such as downsizing, industrial engineering process streamlining, or line item budget reductions?

In a way it seems as though this would be the natural time

to incorporate headcount reductions, removing extra layers of management, and eliminating excess staff capacity. The problem-solving process will probably identify numerous opportunities for expense savings through displacement. One savings bank in California undertook one or two acquisitions several years ago but never dealt with the duplication and excess management structure that resulted. In planning their quality program, they included explicit goals regarding these problems. In other words, they were going to ask their employees to look for ways to eliminate jobs. Society Corporation in Cleveland did much the same thing: While looking for "value added" activities, employees were encouraged to find solutions that deleted lots of jobs, including their own.

Organizational restructure is a key factor of Quality Value Engineering. Streamlining management structure, eliminating duplication in jobs, functions, and activities, and finding more creative ways to structure both people and work are fundamental to the QVE process. QVE is strongly committed to the talent bank, or resource redeployment, concept, whereby displaced persons are retrained or warehoused for future positions, or shrinking by attrition, where an ideal organization is designed and then the company is slowly shrunk to fit it by not replacing jobs that have been found to be unnecessary. No company can expect its employees to be enthusiastic about participating in a project that may eliminate their or their colleagues' jobs, unless a viable safety net—in the form of job security—is provided. A good displacement package, while essential, is hardly equivalent to a job, in most employees' minds.

Therefore, if significant short-term savings are essential, and it is known up front that excess structure is a problem whose solution will provide those savings, it is best to undertake that project first. The idea of "job loss" must be divorced from that of "quality." The caveat to this is that more prework will probably be necessary; the more severe the downsizing, the more prework will be required to overcome its effects, such as Survivor Syndrome, as discussed in Chapter 2. Considering the additional investment in time and money required to recover from a downsizing, the opportunity cost of having to postpone a true quality strategy, the offsetting effects of severance packages, increased turnover (often of the best people), and lowered morale and productivity, it might be best to shelve those downsizing plans and opt for a quality effort. Unless the bank is in a true financial bind, the long-term benefits of quality will far overshadow the short-term costs of carrying the excess for an additional year or so.

The same is true for other types of projects. Most of them involve outside experts coming in and *doing* something *to* the organization, and if they must be undertaken then they should be gotten out of the way first. There should be an adequate amount of time between their completion and the beginning of QVE. Again, the problem-solving section of QVE will probably identify most if not all of the problems and solutions that an outsider could, and others besides that an outsider could never know. The identification process may take a little longer, but it will be just as successful and implementation will be considerably more so, since employees will be carrying out their own ideas.

Many people considering a quality approach are still unclear on the fundamental concept: A quality strategy is a profit strategy. There's no either/or choice: Choose quality, and profits will follow. Undertaking other projects does not "hedge" the quality bet; other projects tend, rather, to interfere with the natural odds in its favor. Do other projects first, do them fast, and try to repair the damage. Then go for quality, and do it right.

NOTES

1. Joseph M. Juran, *Juran on Leadership for Quality: An Executive Handbook* (New York: Free Press, 1989), p. 130.

2. Barry Deutsch, "A Conversation with Philip Crosby," *Bank Marketing*, April 1991, 24.

3. "The Human Side of Quality," National Quality Forum VI, New York City, October 1990.

4. From Jennifer I. Myhre, director of quality performance, American Savings Bank, Irvine, California.

5. We would like to acknowledge and thank Ray Burch, of the Burch Group, and Tony Tosca, of Skopos Corporation, for teaching us this model and how to apply it as part of their excellent Organization Consulting Program.

Chapter 6

How to Implement Quality Value Engineering

This chapter gets into the heart of the QVE process itself; this is really the how-to of the book. The reader must bear in mind one important thought: QVE is a template for problem identification and resolution, but it cannot be simply overlaid onto any and every organization without some modification. How extensive that modification must be depends, of course, on the organization itself.

DATA COLLECTION

By now the external customer surveys should have been distributed; with luck, some results are in. It is time, therefore, to begin the internal data collection process. This will be much easier since there is, of course, more control internally than externally. Three tools are required: the customized dictionary of activities; a writing instrument (preferably a pencil with a good eraser); and a customized survey packet. The groups should be cross-functional and, if data collection is done separately from the workshops, should include employees from all levels of the organization. It is a good idea to have a senior manager explain the data collection procedures and give an introduction to the facilitators, even if they are internal and well known. It lends a little more credibility to the process and is a demonstrable example of management commitment.

The facilitator will explain the contents of the survey packets and give instructions for their completion. Most of it will be self-explanatory and directions should be included in the packet itself, but it is always useful to present them and to give people an opportunity to ask questions. The first page of the packet will ask for demographic and activity-related information. Figure 6.1 is a sample first page. The information in Sections I, II, and V should be filled out by everyone; the information in Sections III and IV is for managers only. For the purposes of this study, a manager is defined as someone who supervises one or more people and in that capacity has major input in—if not ultimate authority over—hiring and firing decisions, performance appraisals, and promotions or salary increases. Project managers, for instance, are not managers if no staff reports directly to them. "Lead" workers, on the other hand, should be included as managers if they meet the above criteria.

The activities information section will require the use of the dictionary. Each person should have a copy but should not make marks in it so that they can be used in subsequent sessions. The participants should be instructed to choose the activities that best describe their jobs, but only those activities that they do at least 5 percent of the time. This results in a little forced distribution, but some people will include every single activity that they do, and it is more important to get the major expenditures of time and money; it is accuracy, not precision, that is wanted. Five percent of the time translates into two hours a week in a 40-hour week, one day a month, or 12 days a year. Participants should look at the cycle of activities in their jobs and determine what length of time is appropriate to consider for purposes of assigning percentages. Operations people will have activities that they perform every single day, while some staff functions are more project-oriented.

The last section of the packet is the internal customer survey. This section of the packet will be different for some participants, as users will be matched with services that they use frequently. This "matching" requirement means that forms

ACTIVITY MEASUREMENT DATA

I.   Your Supervisor's Name _____

II.   Your Name _____   Title _____

      Position _____   I.D. # _____

      Location _____   Shift _____ Salary _____

III. *Managers Only*   IV.   *Managers Only.*
      Supervisors Reporting to You   **Workers** Reporting to You

      _____   _____
      _____   _____
      _____   _____
      _____   _____
      _____   _____
      _____   _____

V.   ACTIVITY DATA

Activity Name	Code	Pct. %	P/S	Activity Name	Code	Pct. %	P/S
1.				11.			
2.				12.			
3.				13.			
4.				14.			
5.				15.			
6.				16.			
7.				17.			
8.				18.			
9.				19.			
10.				20.			

Figure 6.1.   Employee Data Gathering Form

containing evaluations of a given service will have to be distributed to the right group of people. This may be done by preselecting the users and preprinting their names on the correct forms, or by distributing the correct forms to the supervisors of the identified user groups.

Filling out the survey packet will probably take no more than 45 minutes. A wealth of data is provided in a very short period of time, which is what makes this method of data collection so effective. At the end of the session, as each person is leaving, it would be nice to give a gift in appreciation of their attendance. While it needn't be terribly expensive, it should be useful and of high quality. If it can be tied into a theme that the bank has chosen for its process, so much the better.

ANALYSIS OF RESULTS

This is the technical aspect of QVE. The intent of analysis is to provide the organization with a snapshot in time of itself, to identify state-of-the-bank benchmarks, and to put a stake in the ground against which changes can be measured. A number of statistics will be produced that will be useful in their own right but will be even more useful when compared across organizational functions and divisions, and especially when compared through time.

The form of the analysis is "gap analysis." That is, it points out the difference between *what is* and *what should be.* More concretely, it shows the difference between what is demanded and what is produced. Most important in the process is the ranking and prioritizing of gaps in order to take action on them.

There will be results in four analytical areas: service quality measurement (SQM); organization environment analysis (OEA); product and activity measurement (PAM); and automation and technology analysis (ATA). Each product or service that was evaluated will have these four areas of analysis applied to it. SQM will be compiled by the Value Creation Coaches and presented to the Quality Council in order for them to choose which products and services should be addressed first and, therefore, assigned to a Value Creation Team. The data for the other three analyses must be compiled by the coaches and put into a usable form; the actual analysis of the information will be done by the Value Creation Teams during the Dialogues, with assistance, of course, from the Value Added Teams.

Service Quality Measurement (SQM)

SQM points out the gaps between the expectations and perceptions of users, both internal and external. The gaps mirror five dimensions of service quality:[1]

- Reliability
- Responsiveness
- Assurance
- Empathy
- Tangibles

Using a specialized statistical software program, SQM data can produce an internal profile of the employees' perceptions of the company's internal services. These are then compared to their expectations of those services, not as they have always been provided but as they should be provided. Users also rank the importance of the services, and the frequency with which they use them. The result of this analysis is a priority listing of the most severe problems in terms of quality for the products and services evaluated. This list will enable the Quality Council to choose the projects it wants undertaken first. The rest of the analyses will provide supplemental information for determining some of the causes of poor quality in the product or service.

Organization Environment Analysis (OEA)

There are two aspects to the organization environment: structure and culture. The actual structure of the organization can be diagrammed using the information in Sections II–IV of the survey packet. A detailed organization chart can be created showing every manager position. The chart should not be cluttered with staff positions off to the side as in a standard organization chart; staff positions such as assistants or individual contributors should be included in the span of control.

This chart should be annotated with the name, function, location, shift, salary, and span of control of each manager position. The chart should clearly display the layers of management, spans of control, functional groupings, and reporting relationships. Such structural statistics as ratio of managers to workers and cents to manage can be easily calculated.

The chart should make clear where there is excess structure and duplicated functions. Breaking the overall chart down into its component functions or divisions, structural comparisons can be made. Later, the chart will be compared against process or product work flows, to see where organizational factors might be helping or hindering.

The cultural part of the OEA will identify strengths and weaknesses in the organization with respect to the seven variables mentioned before (mission, leadership, human resources, systems, structure, communication, and rewards). As with structure, information about and attitudes toward these variables will be overlaid onto a work flow chart to see where barriers to success reside within the culture of the organization.

Product and Activity Measurement (PAM)

This is the analysis of the activity information in Section V of the survey packet. Its objective is to calculate activity costs by individual, function, and product, as well as for the overall organization. This information will help identify where excessive support work is being performed, where there is duplication of activities and fragmentation of jobs, and where expenditures on activities do not reflect their relative importance to the organization or the product or service being studied.

Doing this analysis correctly requires the use of specialized software.[2] This software can manipulate the activity data provided and produce readable reports that make all information readily available. The software is expensive and, of course, requires someone to run it, although it may be a worthwhile investment if staff is available. Otherwise, the analysis can be simulated in a simplified manner using readily available spreadsheet software; sophisticated personal computer users might want to use a relational database program.

Automation and Technology Analysis (ATA)

This analysis requires the assistance of a technology or systems expert from within the organization who knows what is being used internally and what is available in the market. The purpose of the analysis is to compare the automation tools in place with the service or product provided to determine where there might be a systems problem or a systems solution. This person should also act as an advisor to the Value Creation and Value Added Teams to stimulate their thinking about systems solutions and also to let them know what is technically and financially feasible for the organization.

VALUE CREATION TEAMS

The results of the SQM surveys, presented to and analyzed by the Quality Council, provide the basis for deciding which products and services should be tackled first. The council will probably use such criteria as the volume produced, the severity of the service gaps, and the assessed impact on the bottom line and customers. As the first application of Quality Value Engineering, the council should also consider the likelihood of noticeable results in a relatively short period of time. In trying a new approach it is always best to start with a quick success, to validate the process and provide motivation for the next iteration.

The Quality Council will choose a small number of projects based on these considerations. At least two and no more than four projects should be chosen. Once the products or services have been determined, the Value Creation Teams can be assembled. These can be assigned or be composed of volunteers. They must consist of users and providers of the product or service, must be cross-functional, and should have between six and 12 members; eight is ideal. They should consist of first- and second-level managers. There are several reasons for using this particular group:

- The majority of quality problems are management-related, not worker-related.
- Management commitment is essential to the process.
- These lower level managers are still fairly close to the customer and they will be running the company some day.
- Full participation on the teams requires a bigger outlook than many workers possess.
- The team members must have people reporting to them who can act as Value Added Team members.

There are three orders of business that must be undertaken right away by the Value Creation Teams. One is to acquire a team identity. To some extent, this will only happen slowly and gradually as the group works together for a common purpose over time. However, the process can be speeded up a little by having them assume some of the trappings of a team: a name, a slogan, tee shirts, and mugs proclaiming who they are. Regular team-building exercises in the first three or four Dialogues will also serve to hasten the bonding process.

The second order of business is to determine the leadership of the group. The method of identifying a leader should be left to the team. They might ask that a leader be assigned, they may choose to elect a leader, they may want to rotate leaders. It is possible that they will not want any formal leadership, and the teams can work perfectly well without it. In fact, this is a good time to test the "self-managed work team" concept, if it is not already in place in the organization at large.

The last order of business before actually tackling an assigned project is to organize Value Added Teams. The VATs will assist in researching homework assignments, brainstorming ideas, and generally acting as partners in the problem-solving process. It might be a good idea to have some quasi-social function so that the extended membership can meet each other; in most organizations, it will be the first time for many of them. The team members should also meet with the council to hear first-hand what its role will be, namely, to help and support the teams, to provide advice and resources, and to act as a sounding board for ideas.

At this point, the Value Creation Teams are ready to convene formally and begin their work. They should plan to meet ten times, weekly or biweekly, for approximately six hours each meeting. They will be following an agenda, called the Dialogues, which determines the format of each meeting and assigns homework problems to be completed in the intervening days. The Dialogues, which will be covered fully in Chapter 7, are really the heart of the QVE process. They have two primary purposes: They are a communication vehicle for service users and providers, and they are a problem-solving technique. Although as a methodology they are quite structured, the structure permits and encourages great creativity in analysis, problem identification, and idea generation.

The Dialogues are conducted, with the help of internal or external facilitators, for a period of ten to 20 weeks. Each Dialogue moves the group forward, through data analysis, flowcharting, benchmarking, goal-setting, brainstorming, recommendations, and documentation. The outcome of the Dialogues at the end of the period is an action plan, and the last Dialogue is a presentation of the action plan to the Quality Council. In keeping with the tenor of the program, the teams should be encouraged to be creative in their presentations. The action plans will consist of the following pieces of information:

- SQM, OEA, PAM, and ATA benchmarks
- Detailed recommendations for improvements

- New performance standards and measures
- Discussion of financial and nonfinancial impacts, both positive and negative, and quantified to the highest degree possible
- The resources required to implement the recommendations
- The time frame required to implement the recommendations
- Specific assignments of tasks and responsibilities

The teams will have been in contact with members of the organization as well as with the council to ensure everyone's full understanding, including their own, of the issues involved in solving the problems identified and in implementing those solutions. Not only will teams be working "downward" (organizationally speaking) with their Value Added Teams, but they should also be working "upward" to obtain the cooperation of senior managers in the departments that are involved in the product or service process being studied. And of course they will be working "sideways" with peers in other areas of the organization.

The responsibility of the Quality Council at this point is to review the action plan and ask probing questions. These questions may necessitate additional research or some reworking of various details of the plan. Nothing will be more discouraging to the teams or debilitating to the quality process than to have the plan nitpicked, unduly challenged, or rejected wholesale. The council must keep very open minds and should try not to disapprove anything that does not specifically conflict with the law, regulations, or standard bank policy. In the case of conflict with policy, the council should examine that policy before dismissing the plan; it may be that the policy itself is obsolete or misdirected. With its more strategic outlook, the council may suggest a prioritizing of tasks, but it would be a mistake to direct the process too much. The teams must have the leeway to implement their solutions for the process to have credibility and therefore possibility of success in the organization at large. The council must adopt an attitude of trusting, letting go, and changing. The Dialogues will help ensure that most bases are covered and that agreed-upon solutions are workable.

After the action plan is approved by the Quality Council it should be shared with the members of the departments or functions that will be affected, in other words, with those who will be expected to implement the recommendations of the plan. As stated above, this should not be the first time these people have heard of the proposed changes. There may be some minor changes based on coordination, sequencing, or duplication issues, but agreement for implementing the plan should be the goal of this meeting.

Once the plan is formally approved, it can be summarized on an action plan form, a simple document that clearly shows who is going to do what, when, what the expected results are, and the objective of doing it. It may be useful to format the action plan as a GANTT or PERT chart, or at least as a simple time line. It is more important to have a document that is simple to use than one that is formally correct. The action plan should be distributed to all the people who have assigned tasks, as well as to the members of the Value Creation and Value Added Teams, and the Quality Council. The action plan will serve as a monitoring tool during the implementation period.

DOCUMENTATION, MEASURING, AND MONITORING

The Value Creation Teams must be careful to monitor their progress throughout the Dialogues and the implementation phase, especially in the first go-rounds, but also in subsequent iterations. The purpose of the documentation is to identify and solve process problems such as bottlenecks, working relationships, coordination with the Value Added Teams, and difficulties in the Dialogues. It should focus on the arrived-at solutions to those problems for use by future VCTs. Equally important, the teams should document their successes: what went particularly well, and why, and how other teams might ensure that they repeat the successes. The contents of the documentation should include the following: steps and timing of the project; strengths, weaknesses, barriers, and opportunities; consolidation of the recommendations as initially conceived, as amended, and as ultimately approved; the implementation methodology and schedule; and the probable financial impact. The point of the documentation is twofold: It serves as a resource for the next round of projects and teams, and it provides a record of the process and its outcomes.

Included in the documentation and the action plans will be mechanisms for measuring and monitoring the progress and results of the plans. Some form of action reporting should be designed that is concise, regular, and cross-functional. It may be an expanded form of the action plan itself, or it may be some other document. But however it is conceived, it is absolutely essential that progress be measured faithfully and accurately.

RECOGNITION CEREMONIES

The fun part of implementing a quality program is the recognition ceremonies, and they can be inserted almost any time in the process. A natural time to do it is after the first-round participants on the Value Creation Teams have presented their plans and they have started to have some effect, in order to publicly recognize the efforts and performance of the VCTs. Honoring them in a special ceremony will not only reward their achievement, which by then they will have richly deserved, but will also serve to motivate the next round of participants, as well as to demonstrate the serious commitment that the organization has to its new quality strategy.

There are many possible formats for the ceremonies; they needn't even be consistent from year to year. The format may depend on the culture of the organization, the time of year, and how many participants there will be. Some may opt for an informal summer picnic, softball games, or other outdoor events. Others will want a more formal luncheon or banquet. The format is unimportant. What is important is that the ceremony be bank-wide, out of the ordinary, and very special. It should not be a somber event, but fun and upbeat. It should be held annually, at least.

An example of a formal recognition ceremony is the one given at BancOne Corporation each year. The "Quality of Customer Service Awards Banquet" is held from 10:00 A.M. to 3:00 P.M.. It includes a printed program and menu, a message from the chairman, and a luncheon banquet. They give two to three awards to each of their subsidiaries; the award winners' names are published in the program. Every page of the program is printed with their "Best of the Best" ceremony slogan, reminding everyone of what is being honored.

There is quite a bit of debate as to whether honorees should be given monetary rewards. There will almost certainly be substantial savings associated with most quality-related projects, and there is no reason why the people responsible for generating those savings should not share in them. And if the bank wants to make a tangible demonstration of commitment, there can be no better way than to distribute some percentage of those savings to the Value Creation and Value Added Team members. Not only is this "gainsharing" rewarding and motivating, it only seems fair.

COMMUNICATION

Communication is not just one of the most important components of a quality program; it is probably the most important component. Initially, it is a constant battle to combat the "fad-of-the-month" attitude of the majority of employees; periodic and ongoing communication to all employees throughout the process will be the best weapon in that battle. The more personal it is, the better; and it must be consistent, internally and externally.

There should be two CEO/program sponsor letters: one for the assessment study, and one for the QVE project. This letter should be informative, personal, and inclusive (see Figure 5.2). A followup letter, shown in Figure 6.2, continues that approach into the QVE process itself. It requests, rather than assumes, the cooperation and assistance of the people of the organization. It lets them know what to expect, and this is very important. People don't like change, and they definitely don't like to be surprised by it. If too much static is raised by letting people know too much in advance, then a lot more prework will be necessary before undertaking Quality Value Engineering.

MEMORANDUM

TO:	MY COLLEAGUES
FROM:	PRESIDENT
DATED:	AUGUST 7, 19XX
SUBJECT:	QUALITY VALUE ENGINEERING (QVE) - DATA COLLECTION

What in the world is QVE? Has management lost it? More jargon! Don't they know I am busy and don't have time to do another thing?

If we are honest with ourselves, that is a normal response. The fact is we are busy. More loans, more transactions, more rules, more customers, more inquiries—the list goes on.

There is no question that as a team we are doing a great job. It shows. How else can you explain the lines at our bank when competitors' offices are so quiet? Our problem is we are growing and our customers and competitors are changing. We need to change, to look at the way we do work and learn more about our customers and the competition so we can maintain and reinforce our reputation and its byline—"We're for you." Isn't that a nice problem to have?

How do we—each of us and the directors—continue to meet or exceed customer expectations? How do we stay ahead of the competition? Any answer(s) must be simple. My premise is that skilled, motivated employees providing quality customer service will cause customer satisfaction which causes greater customer retention, less employee turnover and more success. Hopefully, success includes a sense of achievement for each of us as well as the usual financial components of earnings and capital for the bank.

How should we go about improving our understanding of quality? True quality requires a consistent, skillful and timely response to a customer's

Figure 6.2. CEO Sponsor Letter

need. To accomplish this, decisions must be made close to the customer, certainly not in my office. Remember my two rules: "Each of us must have an inquiring mind and must have a healthy disregard for rules." You may say, "But we are a bank, a regulated business! How can we have confusion, even chaos?" I agree with the concern—but in terms of our survival, there is no option. We must change to meet a customer's need or we lose customers, earnings, and ultimately a great place to work.

It is apparent that to be successful we need to:

1) Focus on solving the business problems of the external customer and be action oriented.

2) Obtain more information about the customer and the competition and build our marketing and sales strategies and action plans based upon our goals and our analysis of the situation.

3) Provide a greater learning opportunity for each of us so that we know as much about the business of the bank and about its customers as possible and that we constantly question what, why and how we do what we do.

4) Work to improve the way we do work with a goal—quality.

As some of you may recall, we invited Value Concepts, Inc., to perform a survey which included some fifty interviews intended to gauge our commitment to quality. Based on an analysis of this information, the management team has agreed to pursue excellence through Quality Value Engineering (QVE). It is expected that this initiative should be fun, highly participative and enable us to provide the quality results which all of us want to achieve.

The first step in the QVE process is for Janet and Tom to conduct Data Collection sessions at which they will be able to get information about our organizational involvement, internal service quality and the state of automation and technology. Each of you will be asked to attend a two (2) hour meeting to learn what must be done to achieve quality, what is included in the QVE process as well as instructions on how to respond to the questions which will appear on specially designed forms that will be provided. This will be your first opportunity, but by no means the last, to participate in the QVE process.

It is important to point out that this is a long term project. It is not a "quick fix." We will be counting on each and every one of you to make us more successful. It is through well motivated employees that we will be able to provide quality customer service which will result in customer satisfaction. It is our commitment that this process will lead to our continued success. Most important, it should help each of us to become more creative and innovative than anyone thought bankers could be.

What do I expect from you? Best efforts—honesty—what, why, how questions—commitment. Put another way—Let's tear down the blocks to quality customer service. There will be no magic answers and few easy answers. By working together as a bank team we will be successful.

Questions? Comments? Give me a call.

Figure 6.2. (*Continued*)

More letters should be circulated during data collection, just to keep in touch. At the beginning of the survey a letter from the CEO or program sponsor should be circulated, and at the end of the survey a letter from the facilitators should be distributed. The purposes of the letters are to reinforce what has already been said and to reassure people that this is a user-friendly process that is going to benefit them personally as well as improve the organization as a whole.

There are few practices less conducive to encouraging full participation in a new project than making everyone give information without getting any back. Virtually all employees will have experienced filling out surveys for various organizational studies, never to hear any more about them. They question, and rightly so, the point of giving full and accurate information when they don't know what is going to be done with it. QVE must break that pattern, and the preliminary results should be shared with the entire employee population. They should be informed of the choice of service quality projects; the identification of the Value Creation and Value Added Team members; the time and effort required; the extent that their cooperation is necessary and expected; and the expected objectives six to 12 weeks hence.

Once the recommendations have been approved by both the Quality Council and the affected departments, the action plan should be announced to the entire organization. Even people outside the involved departments may be indirectly affected, and they are apt to be more willing to put up with temporary inconveniences and snafus if they understand the reason. This communication should be particularly upbeat and optimistic. The bank has just completed the first phase of a program that is going to make it number one in quality—and that's exciting! Everyone should be made to feel and share the excitement.

Some organizations will have bad news to share along with the good. This, too, must be communicated. Obviously, private actions will not be announced publicly, but summaries of job losses, job changes, and similar actions should be disseminated in as positive a light as possible. The creation of a talent bank, in particular, should be presented positively—not just as an alternative to displacements and layoffs but as an opportunity for personal growth and career changes for the individuals whom the bank has deemed too important to lose, even though their jobs have been eliminated.

All anticipated changes should be announced as far in advance as possible, and people should be encouraged to respond to those changes. If nothing else, employees can vent their displeasure at having to experience change; more important, valid objections may be raised that were not thought of previously. Most important, people should not experience QVE as something that is done to them. They must perceive themselves as partners in the process. Eventually, everyone will have an active role, but even initially each person is integral to the success of the program by keeping the channels of communication open—and that means both ways.

In addition to internal communications, various outside constituencies need to be informed of what the bank is doing. External communications will go out to such interested parties as the media, the public at large (potential customers), and present customers. Again, the message should be positive: that the bank is undertaking a proactive, innovative project that will benefit everyone associated with the bank. Keep the outside world apprised of progress and successes; brag a little or a lot. The public relations campaign should ensure that the message is consistent and frequent. And if the bank is ever interested in applying for the Baldrige Award, communicating about quality to anyone who is interested in learning about it is a requirement for all winners.

That, of course, raises an interesting issue of giving away information to competitors. No one would willingly forfeit their competitive advantage, and a solid quality program will certainly be that. Obviously, external communications have to be handled with great tact and sensitivity. The Baldrige folks do not, of course, compel anyone to give away trade secrets. MBNA America says, with great confidence, that anyone can come into their facility and see the customer satisfaction measurements, quotations, and signs; it won't do them a bit of good without the culture and people to back them up. That is the key to successful communicating: Competitors can duplicate techniques; they can't duplicate commitment. Project documentation should be located centrally where any employee who wants to can look at it and learn from it. Eventually, an entire library of projects will be formed.

CONTINUING THE QUALITY JOURNEY

Quality is a journey, not a destination.[3] Quality Value Engineering is one step in the journey. Creating the Quality Council, forming the teams, implementing the plans . . . QVE is a process, not a program, that forms a never ending spiral of quality improvement. There must be mechanisms for perpetuating QVE and continuing the quality journey.

One way this is done is by building in Value Creation Team continuity. Going back to the original SQM data enables the next tier of problems to be identified and tackled. New Value Creation Teams can be assembled, but this time one or two experienced members from the previous teams can be included on each of the new teams. That way, reliance on facilitators is reduced, the process becomes more widely disseminated and internalized, and the new members benefit from the trials and errors of the former members. Quality Value Engineering, then, becomes the form of problem-solving for the organization and can be used to address literally any problem. It is impossible that an organization would ever run out of problems or issues to address, given the changing nature of the industry, but even if it did new Value Creation Teams could be used to look at old problems from a fresh perspective. Participation on a Value Creation Team would also be an excellent form of orientation for new employees. The team would benefit from an outsider's view of the organization, and the new employee would certainly get a crash course in the way the organization works and thinks.

Another technique for ensuring continuity is education. All employees should be updated periodically on advances and innovations in the field of quality. Continuing education can take the form of in-house workshops or seminars by outside experts. If a special Quality Department is formed, those employees would be specially charged with keeping themselves and the rest of the organization informed about new theories and techniques. Better yet, employees should be able to contribute to that growing field of knowledge by their own experience. What will likely happen is that employees, as they become more and more involved in quality in their own organization, will take an ever-increasing interest in the subject of quality in general. And they will become a lot less tolerant of poor quality in other areas of their lives.

Yet another way to instill continuous quality improvement is by instituting a formal quality planning process. Quality planning is a serious signal to continuously monitor and improve the quality of the bank. Incorporating it into the MBO or PA process and tying it to bonus and incentive plans guarantee that it will be heeded. One of the goals of the Value Creation Teams is to identify measures and standards for tracking quality performance, so that monitoring quality initiatives becomes a natural part of the improvement process.

NOTES

1. As already mentioned in Chapter 4, we are indebted to Valarie A. Zeithaml, A. Parasuraman, and Leonard L. Berry for this analytical framework as they presented it in their book, *Delivering Quality Service: Balancing Customer Perceptions and Expectations.*

2. We use The Organization Analyst, available commercially from Cheyenne Software, Inc., in Roslyn, New York.

3. Leonard L. Berry credits Mary Rudie of Merrill Lynch with originating this phrase in a 1983 American Marketing Association speech.

Chapter 7

Value Creation Dialogues

QVE relies on data gathered from the bank's staff to produce "state-of-the-bank" benchmarks of service quality and organizational effectiveness. This information contains the specific structural barriers to the ways in which the bank delivers its services to its customers, gaps between what those customers expect and what they perceive they are getting, a current reading of the bank's culture, and the state of its technology. These benchmarks are the basis for the work of the Value Creation Teams.

The technique of value creation Dialogues can be used to form teams and move them through a process of data analysis, idea generation and identification of improvement opportunities and recommendations for acting on them. The basic framework is tried and true, yet much customization is required to make it effective in different banks; and different teams within the same bank require different treatment. Many factors must be taken into account when applying the Dialogues in a bank: culture, financial condition, team composition, the area under study, and other relevant issues that only staff members are aware of.

"A FREE FLOW OF MEANING BETWEEN PEOPLE"

The word "dialogue" is significant. The best definition comes from *The Fifth Discipline* by Peter M. Senge, who termed it "a free flow of meaning between people."[1] The word "dialogue" is better than "discussion," the root of which is a "banging together." "Discussion" is similar to the word "percussion." Musicians must strike percussion instruments like drums, cymbals, tympani, chimes, bells, and piano, to produce the desired sound. Likewise, in typical conversation, people beat their points on others with the hope that they will not hit back.

People seldom engage in true dialogue. They may not listen to each other, or may believe so strongly in their position that they dominate the conversation and do not let the others say anything. If people "discuss" an issue, there are two visible sides being taken. If a person does not listen to what is being said, considering it carefully within the context of the issue at hand, true communication is most likely blocked.

Dialogue, a free flow of meaning, is at the heart of Quality Value Engineering. Value creation Dialogues are designed to allow participants the opportunity to talk with each other about the issues that affect the bank's ability to accomplish its mission and objectives. The Dialogues are designed to encourage communication among people who work in the same organization and who have, or should have, the same goals and aspirations.

What the participants in the Dialogues will come to find out is that it is exciting to get a new perspective, to learn something from someone else, and to establish a common ground where they are all working to achieve the same objectives. Likewise, it is refreshing to have the trust of another and the confidence to say what you think, knowing that it will be treated with respect.

CHECK YOUR EGO AT THE DOOR

Lionel Richie, prior to assembling that wealth of musical talent to create "We Are the World," hung a sign on the door of the studio that read, "Check Your Ego at the Door."

This is what people must do to have true dialogue. They must suspend assumptions, biases, and prejudices which, in reality, are all based on fear—of the unknown, of being wrong, of being different, or of failure. People must develop an attitude of trust and confidence to eliminate those fears and preconceptions of the others, as they begin to break down barriers.

Along with this individual baggage, there are also organizational barriers. Finance wonders why they never get along with the people in marketing. There is competition between retail and corporate banking, which blocks true teamwork and dialogue. No one understands the trust department, but the trust people don't care since they have their own agenda. Everyone is "better" than the people who have to process all the transactions in the operations areas. All of this is typical, but pointless.

Organizations filter communications, stifle cooperation, and may demean the people in them. Managers, check your egos at the door. There is no room for an exaggerated ego on a Value Creation Team or Value Added Team. There is simply too much to do.

UNLESS YOU HAVE A TEAM, YOU CAN'T DO MUCH

Dialogues are a team effort. There is a story about the Boston Celtics in the early 1960s that demonstrates the value of teamwork. Bill Russell, the center, reflected that there were times when complete synergy took over. Each player, he recollected, knew where the others were going to be before the play occurred; the passing was almost unconscious; opposing defenses were rendered helpless. That was the reason, he maintained, for their domination of the National Basketball Association, even though each of the players came from an entirely different background.

A teamwork approach takes advantage of the special skills that each of the members possesses and is especially effective where problems are complex or where they affect several areas of the same organization. For this reason, when the team succeeds, the members succeed as well. They are tackling issues that they normally would not, and although it requires time and effort, achieving the objective makes the extra involvement most worthwhile. There is a pride in the team and in the accomplishment itself.

People at all levels want to do a good job and contribute to the prosperity of the bank. They take pride in being asked what they do and how they would close the gaps. They have some wonderful ideas for improvement. All the bank needs to do is harness that energy into team situations, and with a little coaching and guidance, let them go to work.

> Studies have shown that the decision to change from a traditional management system to one based on quality principles is two to ten times more effective when made by a group as a whole rather than when exhorted by an individual lecturer. Giving a group responsibility for their own goals and procedures truly maximizes the increase in productivity and morale.[2]

It's all based on dialogue, a free flow of meaning between people.

FORMING THE VALUE CREATION TEAMS

The Value Creation Teams consist of representatives from all of the departments in a service delivery system. The teams are goal-oriented, with assignments and tasks to complete and the freedom and authority to act as they deem appropriate. They have the mandate to close the service quality and organizational gaps that affect the bank's customers. This provides a unique opportunity for them to perform; to put their special sets of talents to work; and to have the managerial authority, with their Value Added Teams, to implement effective change.

When the call comes from the Quality Council, the reactions of the recipients are predictable. Some people cannot wait to join a Value Creation Team and start to determine how they can juggle their calendars to find the necessary time. Others provide responses like, "I have too much to do to get involved with that Quality thing. We have too many fires to put out."

The council should encourage people to participate. Its enthusiasm alone should provide that encouragement, but it may find it necessary to "sell" the benefits of being on a team, at least in the first cycle. Membership should not be made mandatory.

The teams consist of managers and supervisors who are responsible for activities and functions within a given delivery system. They should include managers from various staff areas, so that those interfaces can be accounted for and support resources can be made available. Table 7.1 gives one possible composition for two teams, one for a line process and the other for a staff process. Every team should contain at least one member who can act, in a term borrowed from bridge, as the "dummy." Teams need an outsider who can ask the "dumb" questions and open their eyes to engrained idiocies and fresh ideas.

Each one of the team members must be dedicated to the goals of the team and must make the necessary time available to attend meetings, to assemble and lead a Value Added Team, to brief functional management, and to do everything else that had to be done before there was such a thing as a Value Creation Team. Team members must adopt a global view of the delivery system, seeing how their individual pieces of it fit and how this affects the ultimate consumer of the bank's products. In short, there is a lot of work.

Table 7.1   Value Creation Team Composition

Demand Deposit Processing	*Human Resources Employment*
Deposit Operations Manager	Employment Supervisor
Branch Administration Manager	EEOC/Benefits Specialist
Branch Manager(s)	Branch Administration Manager
Corporate Banking Manager	Corporate Banking Manager
Retail Lending Manager	Deposit Operations Manager
Customer Service Supervisor	Loan Operations Manager
Accounting Manager	Data Processing Supervisor
Human Resources Specialist	Information Systems Engineer
Information Systems Engineer	Controller
Return Items Supervisor	Retail Lending Manager
	Trust Department Manager

The teams will have specific, consistent output objectives:

- Strategies, tactics, and direction for closing the service quality gaps
- Recommendations for improving organizational design and effectiveness
- Reduced cost of quality
- Detailed action plans including responsibilities, schedules, tasks, and assignments
- New, dynamic service quality standards

The basis for their improvement work is the information obtained in the employee data-gathering sessions, which has allowed the coaches to develop the various benchmarks (SQM, OEA, PAM, and ATA). Data are a necessity for two reasons. First, the teams need data before they can deal with the issues before them. In many cases, well-intentioned improvement processes fail to reach their potentials because the team members have to deal with undocumented and unsubstantiated perceptions. In QVE, the data that are gathered represent the current situation in terms of service quality, organizational effectiveness, work distribution, and the state of technology.

The second reason for the benchmark data may not be as important in the short term, but should not be regarded lightly. If the bank ever plans to apply for the Malcolm Baldrige National Quality Award, it will be required to demonstrate its progress on the quality journey. The benchmark data, developed at this stage, can serve as the starting point.

As teams begin to meet regularly and the focus becomes clearer, there is a recognizable improvement in the morale and outlook of the members. In the beginning, they may look at membership as a burden, but after a while, they want to attend team meetings, as it is a place where they are encouraged to be innovative and to think about things in different ways.

They also start to talk about quality and begin to integrate the idea that the customer really does come first into their thinking. They have to address service quality and structural gaps, and as they do, the bank starts to institutionalize the concept of quality customer service. Because they have so much data about the quality of their service and they know what specific gaps to address, they can be creative and have fun as they begin to develop strategies for closing them. As the Dialogue process continues, they also measure and report on their progress, and share that success with their Value Added Teams, as the importance of quality service winds its way throughout the organization.

> My unequivocal findings: (1) customers—individual or industrial, high tech or low, science-trained or untrained—will pay a lot for better, and especially *best* quality; moreover, (2) firms that provide quality will thrive; (3) workers in all parts of the organization will become energized by the opportunity to provide a top-quality product or service; and (4) no product has a safe quality lead, since new entrants are constantly redefining, for the customer, what's possible.[3]

VALUE ADDED TEAMS

Members of the Value Creation Teams are responsible for putting together Value Added Teams. It is important, in the empowerment process, to involve as many of the bank's employees as possible and to drive the decision-making as far into the bank as can be done effectively.

The responsibility of Value Added Teams is to provide detailed functional expertise to the problem-solving process. Their existence also forces vertical communication within the functional area which, when combined with the horizontal communication that is occurring within the teams, starts to break down the structural barriers that have prevented the bank from delivering consistently excellent service.

Both the Value Creation and Value Added Teams must be sure of the support of the Quality Council and of the rest of the management of the bank. They must be aware of the talent bank and the concept of resource reallocation, a technique for transferring talent to where it is needed. The success of QVE depends on the creativity and motivation of the bank's people, and they need to be assured that any streamlining will only result in possible reassignment to new and different tasks.

THE DIALOGUES

The Dialogues consist of ten working sessions, each lasting six hours and conducted every two or three weeks. Dialogues must be facilitated by a coaching staff, either in-house advisors or professional value creation consultants, whose task it is to teach the teams about the importance of quality customer service and organizational effectiveness and to guide them through the improvement process. During the sessions, in order to stay focused, telephone calls and other interruptions are discouraged. It is best to conduct the Dialogues off the bank's premises, if possible. Visitors are welcome to observe them, and the members of the Quality Council and Value Added Teams should attend periodically.

The Dialogue framework is designed to provide a logical sequence of activities that need to occur and a suggested format. As different teams will progress at different rates of speed, they may not cover all of the issues and topics in the same Dialogues. If a team does not get to a specific issue by a certain prescribed time, that's okay, since the group felt that something else was more important.

Dialogue One

The first Dialogue provides an introduction to and overview of the Quality Value Engineering process. It is important to inform the teams of what will be expected of them in terms of commitment, effort, and output. The Quality Council empowers them to make changes in the delivery systems; there may be some uneasiness with that assignment. Team members may think that they are not equipped to make those kinds of decisions, but that is only natural as the teams start out. It may help to outline for them the role of the Quality Excellence Council, and it may be useful to have one or more members present to explain it in person. Teams may believe that the primary authority of the Council is "veto power!" This is a very demotivating perception that may take some time to correct. It is preferable to get things straight from the start.

It is appropriate at the first Dialogue to get housekeeping issues out of the way. Various team roles, such as leader and recorder, can be addressed. One of the first tasks they perform as a team is to determine what roles (if any) are necessary and to fill them. The schedule of Dialogues can be presented at this time and adjustments made as necessary, although it should be clearly communicated from the council that the Dialogues take priority over all but business or personal emergencies and already scheduled vacations and conferences.

Ground rules should be presented to the teams. The teams can suggest some of their own to make the sessions function more smoothly. David Cormack identifies eight attitudes of effective team members. These can be considered general "ground rules" for the teams:

1. They are active followers.
2. They know when to give and ask for help.
3. They are willing to be led by any one of the team members, provided the proposal is in the best interests of the group.
4. They take their membership seriously and will assume responsibility on behalf of the group in order to avoid disappointments, problems, or letdowns.
5. They go out and talk to others.
6. They break bad news before it's too late.
7. They pay great attention to keeping up to date.
8. They set their own standards and work to meet them.[4]

Other rules include being on time, doing homework, sharing information and assignments with the Value Added Teams, and being prepared. In the course of the Dialogues it is sometimes necessary to develop other "rules." Team members may waste a lot of time defending their views, justifying their observations, and generally ensuring that they aren't misunderstood or misjudged. It might be helpful to lay out a set of working guidelines that will underlie all communications: (1) make honest observations, without finger-pointing or blaming; (2) team members are not in competition with each other; and (3) there are no dumb questions.

Team-building must be an explicit part of the first several Dialogues. There are many wonderful exercises or "interventions" that enhance and hasten the formation of teams; which ones to use are a matter of personal preference and team composition and progress. The first Dialogue could be initiated with one that serves as an ice breaker and an introduction. In groups of twos or threes, team members interview each other, then report on their "subject" to the group. Any subject is allowed as long as they ask one question: "What do you bring to the team?" Reporting by a colleague is generally funnier and more interesting than self-reporting. Equally important, writing down the answers to the focus question provides a quick analysis of the group. For instance, one team may report attributes such as "an open mind," "communication skills," and "an outside view," while their counterparts on another team may say things like "good analytical skills," "knowledge of the area studied," and "long experience with the bank." Different approaches will be necessary.

Get right to work in the first Dialogue and give the teams real substance. Team members are often surprised, but it is important to demonstrate that these sessions are not a respite from work. They're fun and exciting, but also difficult.

Begin with the cost of quality. It is important to enlist the aid of someone from the finance department. As homework for Dialogue One, team members must research and document the basic processes for which they are responsible and provide estimates of the cost of quality. They must estimate the time spent in preventing, detecting, and correcting poor quality, and attach a dollar value to that time.

Other assignments may be generated from current events in quality and/or banking, appropriate articles, or even television shows. These can provide a point of discussion for the next Dialogue and start to develop common ground of language and knowledge for the team members.

Dialogue Two

The second Dialogue builds on the work of the first. Homework is discussed, team-building continues, and new information is taught. Dialogue Two can be started with a problem-solving exercise that subgroups have to interpret and answer. Groups of three might share their experiences about simple learning situations. Ask them to discover a mutual interest or skill, and then talk about how they acquired mastery of it. It is a simple step to relate those experiences to the one they are now undergoing, namely, Quality Value Engineering. This exercise may alleviate some frustration, yet remind them that they will have to work hard to be successful.

The cost of quality homework should be discussed at length, since this is generally a new concept that many members will have difficulty understanding. The cost needn't be calculated to the penny, as it is the concept that is important, but they should be able to relate the cost and what the drivers are so that not only they, but the entire group, understand it.

Once the concept is understood, the process can be applied to the service being studied. After flowcharting takes place (Dialogue Five, usually), various pieces of the service can be parceled out to the members for a cost of quality analysis. The costs are then accumulated to show the total cost of quality for the service being studied. That, then, is the initial benchmark from which they will set their savings improvement objectives.

New information presented will be "organizing for quality." The teams should be given an overview of bank organization and showed that banks' structures contain the root causes that affect service quality and contribute to the gaps between customer expectations and perceptions.

The team members review the organization reports that have been developed from the data-gathering sessions and begin to identify structural issues. They look for things such as duplication of effort, fragmentation within processes, too many layers of management, or spans of control that are too small or too big. This process allows them to see, for example, how many people are involved in specific activities as "meetings" or "reporting," a number that is surprising to most. They look at individual work profiles of the employees engaged in the process under study, to see what activities are being performed there. Most managers are surprised by this data, as they see things that they and their staff are doing that really don't add any value to the customer.

Adding another dimension to the organizational data are the environmental factors. These give insight into the causes and effects of the structural findings. Both the environmental survey results and the free form comments from the survey forms are categorized into major areas. The primary homework assignment in Dialogue Two is to analyze the environmental results and relate them to the organizational data.

Dialogue Three

The agenda for Dialogue Three is similar to that for Dialogue Two: homework review and discussion, team-building exercises, and a new piece of the information puzzle leading to the thorough analysis of the delivery system under study. The focus of this Dialogue is on service quality.

At this point, the teams understand the cost of quality, how they are organized, and the many activities in which they are involved. They are starting to develop a group identity. They know about teams and the dynamics of groups. In this Dialogue, they will learn about prioritization of alternatives. They will have to make many choices later in the series and will need techniques by which to make them.

The teams learn the importance of quality customer service. They see examples from other industries, as well as from banks, and they talk about their experiences of good and bad customer service, both within their area and outside the bank. This Dialogue can be a lot of fun as the team members recall situations where they were treated very well as well as those times when they were not. It is a natural progression to go from themselves as customers to internal and external customers whom they serve.

It is in this Dialogue that teams learn about the third area of survey results, the service quality gaps. During the data-gathering phase, the bank surveyed samples of employees and customers about the quality of service being provided by the institution through questionnaires designed to measure their expectations and perceptions across the five service quality dimensions. Each survey was scored to calculate the gaps between the service they expected and that which they perceived was being delivered. The results of these surveys become the benchmarks of service quality from which all improvement efforts can begin.

The surveys requested the respondents to rank the five dimensions of service quality in order of importance to them. In this way, the bank is able to determine which of the dimensions is most meaningful to its customers. In banks, "reliability" is typically the most highly prioritized dimension, with "responsiveness" a close second.

When all of the questionnaires are tabulated, the bank has quantified, for a given product or service, the differences between expectations and perceptions within the five dimensions and has prioritized them as well. Table 7.2 demonstrates this comparison. The teams must decide which service gap to tackle first, based on the size and priority ranking of the gaps.

Now that the teams have data about the perceptions, expectations, and priorities of their customers, both internally and

**Table 7.2 Service Quality
Survey Results Demand
Deposit Processing**

Dimension	Gap	Priority
Reliability	−1.352	25.61%
Responsiveness	−1.445	24.81%
Assurance	−1.198	20.86%
Empathy	−0.935	19.01%
Tangibles	−1.390	9.71%

externally, they can begin to deal with the specific issues that cause them. They know what the service quality problems are and can, with their Value Added Teams, begin to correct them, by looking at structure and process design.

They then see the results of the Automation and Technology portion of the data-gathering, which is the final piece of information that they will receive. The ATA contains not only a list of the systems that support the delivery of services to customers, but also how the people that use it feel about them. Systems can be "state of the art," but if they don't help someone do their job, the bank has a problem. At the conclusion of the review of the ATA, they have all of the data required to examine the delivery system itself.

For the homework assignment, the teams are asked to document five examples of the best and worst customer service they have experienced and instances in their own departments where customer service could have been improved.

Dialogue Four

To begin Dialogue Four, the team members present their examples of good and bad customer service. The fun continues as they share their stories; most of them will concentrate on the examples of bad service. They can laugh about it now, but it was a little less humorous when the particular event happened. They are encouraged to see how quality customer service pervades their entire lives, both within the bank and outside of it, and they begin to really understand how important it is. It is important for the teams to begin to understand that the ways they serve their internal customers all along the system result directly in the service quality gaps, a connection that many of them have not made. The culture and conditions of the organization have a direct bearing on the way customers are treated.

In the commercial loan processing department of one bank, customers complained of slow response time. The environmental study revealed a lack of leadership, poor communication, the inability to get anything done, and general frustration with the whole process. These aren't very good marks, but they were only symptomatic of the real problem: increased volume. The number of applications had increased by 35 percent over a two-year period, and because the bank wasn't keeping standards and measures, they didn't realize it and were falling farther and farther behind. The problem was also reflected in the organization reports. To compensate for what seemed like a lack of control, more and more manager positions were added, only exacerbating the problem as communication slowed and duplication of effort increased.

Quality Value Engineering gets to root causes like these and treats them, not the symptoms that they produce. It is not enough to say that, for example, responsiveness is poor; teams must be able to ferret out the real reason for that perception—in structure, work design, and environment—and deal with it.

In order to do that, they have to understand the entire process. So the next step is to explain how to flowchart the basic activity for which each of the team members is responsible. If there is someone within the bank who is familiar with flowchart symbols, it is wise to have that person work with the team members to insure consistency across the entire function. The initial flowchart becomes another benchmark from which the teams can measure progress.

The homework is to prepare a flowchart of the delivery system. Team members may want to work individually on this task, or they may choose to work in groups. The Value Added

Teams must become involved in this exercise, especially those in the areas under study.

Dialogue Five

The really hard work begins in Dialogue Five. The teams have enough information to construct the service quality connection, which is simply the linkage of everything they have been given before. This is where they understand that the service quality gaps are only the manifestation of problems within the delivery system itself which, in turn, start with the basic organization structure.

In the discussion of the homework assignment, members of the teams present an explanation of their flowcharts and take the others through all of the steps involved in their piece of the process. When all have finished, there is one large and complete flowchart on the wall that describes the entire process in detail. The purpose of this exercise to educate each of them as to all of the steps in the process of delivering their particular service to their customers. It is the entire delivery system that counts, and the teams must understand how what they do, individually, affects the others.

The remainder of this Dialogue will be spent in correcting and fine tuning the flowchart. It may be a good idea to invite Value Added Team members to explain the details of various steps in the process. Value Creation Team members may not ask questions except to clarify their understanding of the process as it exists. The output of this Dialogue is a comprehensive flowchart that represents the current system.

Dialogue Six

The sole purpose of Dialogue Six is to understand the process. The flowchart hangs on the wall, and each of the team members is required to explain the steps involved and the reasons behind them. They not only may but must challenge the reasons for performing steps that appear illogical, unnecessary, duplicative, or counterproductive. Members from within the process may explain, but must not justify or defend. The coach's role is critical at this point on many fronts: to keep the discussion on track, to prevent attacking, and to encourage the free flow of information among members.

Overlaying the flowchart should be the additional pieces of information that the teams have at their disposal—structure, activities, and environment. Detailed analysis is not appropriate now, but linkages that appear should be noted for future reference and possible action. What is critical to the process is that they begin to realize that they are part of an entire system, and because they have data, they can look at the problems logically and without blame to set a course for solving them together.

Dialogues Seven–Nine

The teams can now begin to work on improving the process. Accordingly, the first task is to identify the "moments of truth" on the flowchart. These are defined as the places along the route where the bank comes into direct contact with the customer. It includes things like opening accounts, whether in the bank or in the customer's home; taking loan applications; checking account statements; ATMs; tellers; customer service representatives; and any time that the customer comes in contact with the bank. These "moments" are the places where the bank *must* provide superior service.

The second points to be identified are those relating to the cost of quality, whether they be prevention and detection techniques, or those that are incurred in the correction process. Through this exercise, they can ask questions about the preventive techniques in place at every "moment of truth" to ensure that customers perceive that the highest quality service is being delivered. They can also begin to see where detection techniques, such as checking statements to see that they are right, may have little bearing on service delivery. These, then, become candidates for elimination since they add no value to the process and may even detract from it.

After the group has reviewed the entire flowchart, understands the service quality gaps, sees the structural issues that get in the way of quality customer service, calculates the resultant cost of quality, and recognizes the environmental conditions, the fun really begins. It is now time to put it back together, to re-engineer it, and to eliminate the things that have detracted from it.

This is the part of the Dialogue series where teams can begin to ask, "What would happen if we did this?" or "Why can't we change that?" As ideas are generated, they are documented and become the proposals that the team members take to their Value Added Teams. It is the job of the VATs to evaluate the various impacts of the alternatives in terms of their transaction flows and the effect on their customers. This is where the empowerment of the teams is crucial. They must have the freedom to innovate, be creative, and make the appropriate decisions.

As ideas are accepted and rejected, a new transaction flow begins to take shape. The teams are encouraged not to think about the potential consequences of resource reallocation opportunities, but about the ways in which the service quality gaps can be reduced to the point where customer perception exceeds expectation. They are not to think about capacity issues or be limited to current technologies. They are only to think about service to both internal and external customers.

The term for this is "process diagramming," and the purpose of it is to reassemble the delivery systems without those things that the customers do not need and with things that will improve service quality and structure. Since the teams know the transaction process so well, they are able to see the inefficiencies that were built into the previous system and can redesign them out of the new one.

Of the utmost importance is documentation of the new process as compared to the tasks and actions that were done previously. There are three reasons for this. First, removing tasks and activities from the delivery process will mean that the bank will have some excess human capacity. Anyone whose job was dependent on those unnecessary tasks will be transferred to the talent bank for relocation to other positions. Some center-post in the organization, probably the human resources department but possibly the council, the quality department, or some other group, will need to track this procedure.

Second, the teams must calculate the economic impact of the changes. It has had its financial target since early in the process and, as the transaction flow has been simplified, there will be cost savings. Documentation of the new process costs allows them to be compared against the original product and activity benchmarks so that they can begin to see the economic benefit that has been achieved.

Third, the teams can begin to set quality standards. They must identify appropriate measures within the delivery system and determine the standards against which these measures will be compared to gauge the quality improvement of the service. These measures and standards should be incorporated into the performance measurement system used at the bank and tied to individual and group reward systems.

Dialogue Ten

Toward the end of the Dialogue process, the action plan begins to take shape. The plan will contain the improvements to be made, the schedule, the persons from the teams (or outside the teams) who are to be responsible, the financial impact, and the new quality standards. It will include the resources required to implement the changes and a description of the mechanisms that will be used to ensure that progress is being made.

By the time the plan is formulated, team spirit is very evident. There is a pride in accomplishment and a sense of belonging to something that was positive and creative. It is at this point that the teams develop their presentation for the Quality Council, and they are encouraged to be creative in the approach that they use.

Presentation packages are to be prepared and delivered a

couple of days before the Quality Excellence Council meeting and should contain a description of the process under study; the original benchmarks (SQM, OEA, PAM, and ATA); the changes they recommend; and the impacts that they will have. The teams also communicate the financial improvement impact to the financial people who will be measuring progress toward that goal. MIS is prepared to support the recommendations. Human resources is prepared to manage the talent bank. Marketing knows the message to be communicated to the customers that will be affected, if any, and can begin drafting those materials.

The actual presentations to the Quality Council can take many forms, depending on the culture of the bank. The teams have worked hard, have achieved some fine results, are proud of what they have done, and need to be recognized for their achievements.

IMPLEMENTATION

Once the Quality Council has endorsed the plan, the teams may begin to implement it through Value Added Teams. Organizational moves can be made, taking resources from areas where there is excess capacity and retraining them for the areas in which they are needed to satisfy customer demand. The measurement system becomes operational. There must be continued management of the tasks and assignments that were identified as critical to closing the service quality gaps.

During this implementation phase, the teams will meet at least monthly to have dialogue about their progress. They may feel, at the outset, that they need to meet more often. Quarterly, they report to the Quality Council on their progress.

As improvements are made, resources reallocated, and structures streamlined, there will be expense savings, from which the teams may be rewarded. The percentage doesn't really matter, whether it is 5 or 50 percent, but there should be some compensation for a job well done. This reward should be applicable to the Value Added Teams in recognition of their participation.

> The best-run and most successful companies in America do not think in terms of victories and defeats, or shining moments, or last minute saves, and do not count on regulations or referees. Instead, they think in terms of staying power, dedication to quality, and an endless effort to be better than they have been, and they see change as their only constant, count on their own ability to adapt to the world, rather than expecting the world to adapt to them.[5]

The Value Creation and Value Added Teams aren't done, just because they have completed a series of Dialogues, identified and implemented improvements in the way the bank services its customers, saved the organization some money, and received some rewards of their own. No, the process doesn't end there.

Members of the teams will be asked to serve on other ones, perhaps as leaders or facilitators. They will be asked to share their experience with others in the organization and to provide guidance and advice. They are the champions of service quality, the evangelists that Chuck Aubrey of BancOne talks about. They are living proof of what can happen when management lets go of its control systems and its bureaucracies and allows people to service their customers and each other.

They will have learned the importance of structure and environment and how they affect service quality; they will never look at the organization the same way again. More important, they have made a contribution of real value to the bank, by determining the expectations of its customers and designing ways to satisfy them. This is job enrichment; it is creative and entrepreneurial; and it is fun.

The Dialogues have given the teams a chance to think and to learn, to share ideas, and to build an atmosphere of trust. They have given the participants the tools with which to approach and solve complex business problems jointly and without blame. And they have turned the organization upside down, focusing on customers and concentrating on service quality as the bank's only strategy.

Once a bank has come this far, it may start thinking about comparing itself to other world-class quality organizations. The way to do that in this country is to apply for the Malcolm Baldrige National Quality Award.

NOTES

1. Peter Senge, *The Fifth Discipline* (New York: Doubleday, 1990), p. 240.

2. Joseph J. Gudfreda, et al., "Employees' Involvement in the Quality Process," in *Total Quality: An Executive's Guide for the 1990s* (New York: Richard D. Irwin, 1990), p. 164.

3. Tom Peters, *Thriving on Chaos* (New York: Alfred E. Knopf, 1987), p. 68.

4. David Cormack, *Team Spirit* (Grand Rapids: Zondervan Publishing House, 1989), pp. 37–38.

5. Warren Bennis, *Why Leaders Can't Lead* (San Francisco: Jossey-Bass, 1990), p. 100.

Chapter 8

The Malcolm Baldrige National Quality Award

We were presenting "The Cost of Quality" to the spring 1991 conference of the National Association of Bank Cost and Management Accounting (NABCA) when a question that we really hadn't prepared to ask came to mind.

"Does anyone know what the Malcolm Baldrige National Quality Award is?" There was a stillness in the room, followed by that interminable shuffling of papers that indicates a search for the answer. After a few seconds, a hand went up in the very back of the room.

It was an old friend and colleague from First Interstate Bank of California, Richard Paegelow. "I think it's some award for quality," he responded.

"Did anyone else know that?" we asked.

The room was quiet, but soon Richard spoke again. "I wouldn't have known about it either, except that we talked about it when you guys came to First Interstate a month ago to interview me for your book."

Until Cadillac began to advertise that it won a Baldrige Award in 1990, very little had been written or said about it; but that is changing. Companies all over the United States are becoming aware of the importance of the Baldrige and what it stands for as they continue to search for a way to compete in the 1990s. The banks can learn from it, too.

WHAT IS THE MALCOLM BALDRIGE NATIONAL QUALITY AWARD?

On January 6, 1987, Congress passed Public Law 100-107, the Malcolm Baldrige National Quality Improvement Act, named for Malcolm Baldrige, secretary of commerce from January 1981 until his death in a rodeo accident on July 25, 1987. Approximately one month later, August 20, 1987, the bill was signed into law by President Ronald Reagan.

The act recognizes the challenge to American business by foreign competition and the decline of American productivity. It acknowledges the high cost of quality and the linkage of improved quality with lower cost and increased profitability. It outlines a program of quality improvement, including:

- Strategic planning
- Improved management understanding of quality control techniques
- Management-led and customer-oriented quality standards
- A national award giving special recognition to those enterprises the audits identify as the very best

The award was established to stimulate and recognize quality improvement by providing guidelines and criteria that organizations could use to assess their quality achievements. Award winners could be called upon to help other businesses improve quality by sharing with them information and techniques they had developed that had enabled them to win the award.

The Baldrige Award is given annually to American companies that demonstrate the highest level of quality performance in the country for the previous year. The Baldrige Award is administered by the Department of Commerce's National Institute of Standards and Technology (NIST). Its purpose is threefold:

- To promote quality awareness
- To recognize quality achievements of U.S. companies
- To publicize successful quality strategies

The award has the full support of the White House. The honors are given there, and President Bush is quoted on the front cover of the award application guidelines, saying, "The improvement of quality in products and the improvement of quality of service—these are national priorities as never before."

In one of the first articles ever written about the Baldrige Award, Jeremy Main of *Fortune* wrote:

> The prize has no monetary value. It's a gold-plated medal encased in a crystal column 14 inches tall. Yet a lot of CEOs would give away a whole lot of layers of vice presidents to win the thing.
>
> In the three years since Congress created the Malcolm Baldrige National Quality Award, it has become *the* standard of excellence in U.S. business.[1]

American industry has taken the challenge seriously, especially in the manufacturing sector, but it is very difficult to achieve world-class quality and perhaps even harder to win the Malcolm Baldrige National Quality Award. Table 8.1 gives an idea of just how hard it is.

Of the 407,000 applications requested over the last four years, only 0.08 percent have actually been filled in and returned. There has been speculation as to the reason for this falloff, with the most accepted reason being that many companies are very surprised when they see the breadth and depth of the examination categories, decide they cannot win, and do not apply.

No bank has ever won a Baldrige, and before Federal Express won the Baldrige in 1990, there was some debate as to whether or not service companies could be measured by the examination categories. One published view argued that the number of defective television sets that customers take back to the store can be counted, but "you can't count the number of bank depositors who walk away from the teller's window steaming with resentment."[2]

Table 8.1 Malcolm Baldridge National Quality Award Statistics

Year	Applications Requested	Applications Returned	Percent Returned	Number of Winners	Names of Winners
1988	12,000	66	.55	3	Commercial Nuclear Fuel Division of Westinghouse Electric Corporation; Motorola, Inc.; Globe Metallurgical
1989	65,000	40	.06	2	Xerox Corporation; Milliken & Company
1990	180,000	97	.05	4	Cadillac Motor Car Division; IBM Rochester; Wallace Co., Inc.; Federal Express Corporation
1991	150,000	106	.07	3	Marlow Industries; Zytec Corp.; Solectron Corp.

Most of the discussion that took place in the late 1980s arose from the fact that most service companies had not adopted service quality standards and therefore were assumed to be behind their manufacturing counterparts. There has been a continual effort to make the guidelines more applicable to the service sector. The categories now apply to both. They should be further expanded to include measurement and evaluation of financial performance, organizational improvements, and the focus on the long term.

THE COMPETITIVE EDGE

As the American trade deficit continued to mount in the 1970s and "Made in America" meant less than it ever had, members of the Administration and Congress were troubled by the quality issue. They had seen the Japanese rebuild their devastated country after World War II by focusing on quality of products and services. America actually seemed to be slipping behind in the world marketplace. What was Japan's secret?

Using statistical process control techniques developed in the United States, the Japanese began to reverse their reputation for products that would not last and are now in a position of world dominance, especially in the electronics and automobile industries. Maybe, thought the American politicians, if the Japanese can do it, we can, too. But there would have to be a focal point, a lightning rod, to get American management's attention. It would be difficult simply to tell American companies that they were producing poor quality goods and services without giving them an incentive to start thinking differently. The Japanese had established the Deming Prize many years ago to recognize companies that produced superior quality by following Deming's techniques. Why not give American companies that demonstrate world-class quality an award, similar to the Deming Prize? Thus was the Baldrige Award created.

There are a handful of American companies that have consistently put quality first as a corporate mission. The winners of the award fall into this category. Motorola suggests that it has had a formal quality improvement effort for some 40 years. Globe Metallurgical's quality effort was so engrained in its culture that Vice President Ken Leach was able to complete the application for the Baldrige Award over a weekend using data and information that the company produced on a regular basis. Quality assurance started at Westinghouse in the 1960s and 1970s and became a competitive strategy in the early 1980s. Xerox is another prime example. In 1982, when a customer went to make a copy on a Xerox machine, there was a 90 percent success rate. For every nine good copies, there would be one bad copy. Today that success rate is 98 percent.

Why did these companies begin to focus on quality? The reasons were varied but the major one was *competition*. Advances from foreign competition were beginning to erode market share and profits, and they had to find a way to regain what was being lost. The increasingly global marketplace no longer afforded companies a captive national customer base.

Quality and focus on the customer are the only ways that American business will be able to beat the competition. Companies in various industries are beginning to use the Baldrige Award guidelines as the model for their own quality journeys. These companies want to be known for their commitment to quality. Not only is that good marketing, but also, high quality and low cost go hand in hand, and that adds up to increased profitability. These enterprises are proud to admit that they are focusing on quality, even if they have come up short on winning the Baldrige Award. Since there can be only two awards in each of three categories (manufacturing, service, and small business), the odds against winning are huge. But that's not the point, since winning the award is a secondary objective.

The first and foremost objective is to have a complete understanding of the demands of customers and delivering the services that they want at the quality level they require. The Baldrige examination criteria can help companies get there.

Aleta Holub of First Chicago says, "We are using the Baldrige criteria as a self-assessment tool to help us identify not only our strengths, but also opportunities for improvement."[3] Jack Kucler of Society National Bank said that their initial assessment would take at least three months, perhaps longer, and that it would be the basis for a corporate quality improvement plan; ultimately, they may or may not decide to apply for the Baldrige.[4]

Although the Baldrige is that lightening rod that has begun to focus American industry on quality and customer satisfaction, a company does not have to win it to be world-class. Some of the companies that have made it public that they want to be known as quality organizations, yet have not won the award, are Cummins Engine, Next, Texas Instruments, 3M, Corning, Paul Revere Insurance, GTE Telephone, and L. L. Bean. In fact, there are a lot of banks that want to be known that way, including MBNA America, BancOne, and First Tennessee.

KEY CONCEPTS IN THE AWARD CRITERIA

Certain essential concepts are the foundation for the award. The application guidelines state:

- Quality is defined by the customer.
- The senior leadership of businesses needs to create clear quality values and build the values into the way the company operates.
- Quality excellence derives from well-designed and well-executed systems and processes.
- Continuous improvement must be part of the management of all systems and processes.
- Companies need to develop goals, as well as strategic and operational plans to achieve quality leadership.
- Shortening the response time of all operations and processes of the company needs to be part of the quality improvement effort.
- Operations and decisions of the company need to be based on facts and data.
- All employees must be suitably trained and developed and involved in quality activities.
- Design quality and defect and error prevention should be major elements of the quality system.
- Companies need to communicate quality requirements to suppliers and work to elevate supplier quality performance.

Many of these guidelines are not understood or practiced in America's banks, which has led to the belief, on the part of customers, that quality bank service is an oxymoron. Most banks are not focused on these concepts and objectives.

DATA: THE MORE THE BETTER

Applicants for the award must be able to show evidence of progress in all of the examination categories, starting with

Table 8.2   Malcolm Baldrige National Quality Award Examination Categories and Items

Examination Categories/Items' Maximum Points	
1.0 Leadership	**100**
1.1 Senior Executive Leadership	40
1.2 Quality Values	15
1.3 Management for Quality	25
1.4 Public Responsibility	20
2.0 Information and Analysis	**70**
2.1 Scope and Management of Quality Data and Information	20
2.2 Competitive Comparisons and Benchmarks	30
2.3 Analysis of Quality Data and Information	20
3.0 Strategic Quality Planning	**60**
3.1 Strategic Quality Planning Process	35
3.2 Quality Goals and Plans	25
4.0 Human Resource Utilization	**150**
4.1 Human Resource Management	20
4.2 Employee Involvement	40
4.3 Quality Education and Training	40
4.4 Employee Recognition and Performance Measurement	25
4.5 Employee Well-Being and Morale	25
5.0 Quality Assurance of Products and Services	**140**
5.1 Design and Introduction of Quality Products and Services	35
5.2 Process Quality Control	20
5.3 Continuous Improvement of Processes	20
5.4 Quality Assessment	15
5.5 Documentation	10
5.6 Business Process and Support Service Quality	20
5.7 Supplier Quality	20
6.0 Quality Results	**180**
6.1 Product and Service Quality Results	90
6.2 Business Process, Operational, and Support Service Quality Results	50
6.3 Supplier Quality Results	40
7.0 Customer Satisfaction	**300**
7.1 Determining Customer Requirements and Expectations	30
7.2 Customer Relationship Management	50
7.3 Customer Service Standards	20
7.4 Commitment to Customers	15
7.5 Complaint Resolution for Quality Improvement	25
7.6 Determining Customer Satisfaction	20
7.7 Customer Satisfaction Results	70
7.8 Customer Satisfaction Comparison	70
Total Points	**1,000**

benchmarks from which the journey started and continuing to where it is today.

"The exam looks for data," said Wayne Cassatt, deputy director of the Baldrige Award. "We really like to see at least three years of data. Five would be better. The more we have, the better able we are to judge the overall quality of the company."[5]

Each of the seven examination categories is made up of subsections that are scored by the examining staff. The total point score, then, is used to rank the applicants against each other as the competition to find the best two companies in each category continues.

Table 8.2 shows how the points are distributed among the various categories. Customer satisfaction is the most important, accounting for 30 percent of the entire point score.

COMPLETE, NEVER-ENDING FOCUS ON THE CUSTOMER

Baldrige applicants must document their achievements in seven examination categories.

Leadership (100 points)

The objective of the leadership category is to examine the vision of the senior executives of the company and the ways in which they translate those beliefs about excellence of performance into daily activities, the culture, and the management of the organization. A quality institution has a leadership style that lives it and breathes it every day—walking the talk, inside the company and out.

> We believe in it top to bottom, from cleanliness to treating people fairly. It's everyone's responsibility, and that's never changed. Mr. [Charles] Cawley [the chairman and CEO] is the driving force. It's a complete, comprehensive, never-ending commitment to a customer focus. The message is consistent in every detail in the organization. From the food in the cafeteria to how the pictures are hung. No inconsistency.[6]

The Baldrige examination demands evidence of the ways in which these values and beliefs are carried over to the company and the community at large. Not only is it important for everyone in the company to participate in activities outside the company, but they must carry the quality commitment with them as well—local or national; from trade association to hospital board; from church group to the classroom. It looks at leadership in safety, health, ethical business practices, and environmental protection. The commitment to quality doesn't stop at 5:00 P.M.

Information and Analysis (70 points)

The leadership category addresses concepts and ideas, and the processes through which they are integrated into the company's daily activities. The second category, Information and Analysis, shows how commitment to quality and the demand for customer satisfaction really begin to drive the entire organization. The application guidelines state:

> The *Information and Analysis* category examines the scope, validity, use, and management of data and information that underlie the *company's overall quality management system*. Also examined is the adequacy of the data, information, and analysis to support a responsive, prevention-based approach to quality and customer satisfaction built upon "management by fact."[7]

The guidelines talk about the "quality management system," not the general ledger, the MCIF, or the item-processing system. The assumption is that all systems are integrated parts of the all-encompassing "quality management system." Therefore, banks must conduct an evaluation of all systems in the way they support the entire business, from planning, to day-to-day operations, to the determination, measurement, and improvement of current quality levels.

Besides looking at how the systems support the organization, the award also requires the company to compare its performance against the benchmarks of other world-class organizations. There must be a sound approach to the selection of specific ones to ensure that the comparisons are being made against the very best in all applicable categories. For example,

> IBM, a leader in the use of benchmarking techniques, compares itself to DEC in the work station business, Canon in the photocopier market, L. L. Bean in warehouse operations, John Deere in service parts logistics systems, and Ford in assembly automation processes. The company has even studied the Federal Reserve's bill-scanning procedures and Citicorp's document-processing activity to learn better methods for performing these tasks.[8]

What does that mean for the banks? They must get away from thinking that their business is unique. The bank is a processor and distributor of services, marketing to wholesale and retail customers locally, nationally, and internationally. They have processes and operations that are similar to those of many other service providers, and they can learn from all of them, not just other banks. For example, the bank might compare how customers are handled in the branches with the way Taco Bell serves its patrons so quickly and efficiently, or contrast its marketing and advertising approaches with that of American Express. It might look at the way L. L. Bean resolves customer complaints, Procter & Gamble's new product development, or AT&T's credit card operations.

Banks must obtain appropriate and relevant information and be able to analyze it to support the company's quality objectives. There is a subtlety here. Most bankers don't have the *information* they really need to manage the business but *data* from the past.

> All you give me is a snapshot of the last thirty days and the year, compared to a plan that may or may not be any good. What can I do with it? It's like baseball. If my kid makes an error, should he dwell on it? Seems unproductive to me. The only thing he can do is go on and make the next play.[9]

Bankers have to prepare for the changes that are sure to occur, and they must have the data and information necessary to do that. State Street Bank & Trust has adopted an activity-based cost accounting (ABCA) system to help managers understand the relationships of cost, transaction volume, and profitability. SunTrust has done the same thing. Not coincidentally, both banks are showing some very high returns.

Strategic Quality Planning (60 points)

We plan for quality, based on the cost of quality. It becomes a real part of the annual tactical plan. If we want to have world-class quality, we have to plan for it and then measure to see how we are doing.[10]

Not only does the bank have to show that its leaders are active in the quality effort and that the systems provide usable information, but it must plan for strategic quality improvement.

The word "strategic" implies "long-term" and means that current efforts need to be combined with a view of how customer demand will be satisfied several years in the future in terms of economic conditions, political situation, and technological advances. The bank will have to know what the customer wants and will have to plan ways to find out, and management will have to plan the ways it will achieve quality leadership and how it will downstream those plans into tactical and operational ones.

As a practical example of goal-setting, Motorola, a 1988 winner of the Baldrige, has a stated strategic objective of achieving *six sigma*. That means 3.4 defects out of every million parts or, more positively, getting it right 99.9999997 percent of the time. Its tactical and operational plans are designed to achieve that standard which, when accomplished, will most likely be raised again.

At Cadillac, the Business Plan is the Quality Plan. The plan is designed to ensure that Cadillac is the "Standard of the World" in all areas of quality and customer satisfaction. The business planning process accomplishes three things: 1) It drives the annual review of Cadillac's Mission and Strategic Objectives; 2) it guides internal processes; and 3) it builds discipline into the development and achievement of specific short-term and long-term quality goals.[11]

This is the point where many organizations that request copies of the application guidelines realize how serious the Baldrige process really is. This is the time when they realize what world-class quality really means and start to retreat from earnest consideration of the actual application. "The Malcolm Baldrige Award sets a very high stretch standard for the country," says Curt Reimann, director of the Malcolm Baldrige National Quality Award and associate director for quality programs at the National Institute of Standards and Technology.[12]

Human Resource Utilization (150 points)

In this category, the Baldrige review process measures how well the bank develops and makes full use of the potential of the workforce; how the culture is directed toward and devoted to employee involvement and participation; whether quality leadership is at the forefront; and the way in which growth of all employees and the organization is fostered.

All that differentiates a bank these days is the ability of its people. How do banks communicate quality to customers? Bob Lias, vice president of BankOne, Cleveland, says, "That's easy. You have to have quality people and quality service. Both."[13] It's simpler than that: If you have quality people, you will almost certainly have quality service. Of course, getting quality people is the trick. However, there tends to be a happy spiral in pursuing quality: A quality company attracts quality people; quality people enhance the quality of the company.

The Baldrige examination evaluates the bank's ability to match its human resource strategies with its overall quality objectives. It looks for things like training, empowerment, recognition, and development, and at the strength of its efforts to provide them.

The examiners are interested in documented evidence of how the bank's human resources policies and practices foster continuous quality improvement and want to see increased employee involvement all over the bank. They also review how human resources plans contribute to overall quality plans, and then they judge the effectiveness of those plans.

Ever since W. Edwards Deming published *Out of the Crisis* in 1981, employee involvement has been emphasized. People like to contribute, and since nobody knows more about the job that's being done than the people who are doing it, they are the resources that can make quality happen—or not.

Continued education and training are essential, both in technical skills and in the importance of quality and customer service. BancOne, for example, conducts training classes for its people in the importance of bringing daily processes under control and improving them. Part of their planning revolves around the number of people they can train in a given year. Quality education is now a part of new employee orientation as well, which demonstrates how important they think it is.

Another critical element of the Human Resource Utilization category is reward and recognition. People like to be singled out for their achievements, whether individually or as part of a winning team. Their performance should be measured, not only on the basis of financial results, but on their quality accomplishments as well. All too often, performance systems are geared to financial and productivity goals when they should be directed to customer satisfaction and service quality improvement.

One motivating factor that is sometimes overlooked is the way in which the company's environment contributes to morale. Companies now offer fitness programs, counseling assistance, day care, and nonwork-related education, all of which contribute to the growth of the employees. These investments are repaid with increased loyalty and dedication and with reduced costs in areas such as absenteeism. Furthermore, people like to work, and are more productive, in clean, well-lit, and adequate space, with the proper tools to enable them to fulfill their responsibilities. The Baldrige examination process looks at this "tangible" side of the business as well.

Not only does the company benefit from involving the people, but there is individual growth as well. "'To me, the single most exciting aspect of the quality process is its impact on people,' comments John Wallace [CEO of Baldrige winner

The Wallace Co., Inc.]. 'It builds tremendous motivation and pride.' "[14]

According to Reimann, "An organization's continuous improvement is reflected not only in quality results, but in renewed motivation in employees."[15]

Quality Assurance of Products and Services (140 points)

The old definition of quality assurance focuses on spotting defects. The new definition says that quality has to be built into the product or service, not inspected out. The idea of quality assurance is to prevent mistakes before they occur.

This Baldrige category examines the ways in which the company builds quality into products and services through the design of its delivery processes and systems. The Japanese call it "concurrent engineering." It begins with the customer defining what the product or service should be and involves everyone within the company who will have anything to do with it. Groups like Value Creation Teams, consisting of people from all functional, product, and market areas, meet to evaluate current quality levels and customer demand and then design their organizations and delivery systems to meet them. They must consider the effects of their individual activities on the next group within the entire delivery system, making sure that they provide exactly what is expected, setting standards against which to measure their performance. Most banks don't do this.

One bank was very proud of a program in place in the branch system that rewarded tellers who were able to keep dissatisfied customers from closing their accounts. Each time that happened, the teller was given $5 and a commendation from the head of the retail division. Many $5 awards were being given out, and the bank was pleased that tellers were doing such a great job at keeping customers from closing accounts. No one had considered the reason that customers were even thinking of closing their accounts in the first place! They had not thought about what was happening in other parts of the bank that would cause them to take this drastic action. They didn't survey their customers to find out what the problem was, see if there was a pattern, and work with whomever was causing it to fix it. The $5 checks were the wrong answer to a question that hadn't even been asked.

Quality assurance requires review and analysis of the concurrent engineering process itself. The bank has to have measures in place within the process to determine the times and places that there are exceptions and deviations from the plan.

The Quality Assurance category addresses the ways in which the company knows that its products and services are being delivered to the customer's satisfaction. It integrates continuous improvement goals into daily work routines, in staff and line areas as well as in operational ones. It also examines the methods by which these processes are improved. These reviews consider the means (surveys, audits, process reviews) the company uses, the frequency, and the effectiveness of the methods they use.

The process is complex, comprehensive, and must be documented. The application guidelines use terms like "knowledge preservation" and "knowledge transfer," which mean that the bank documents everything with respect to quality improvement and makes those materials available to those who would follow. BancOne uses its mainframe Quality Management Information Control System to document its improvements, having the subsidiary banks upload and download their information. It's expensive at the beginning, says CQO Chuck Aubrey, but as the people use it more, the costs become more reasonable.

Quality Results (180 points)

Assuming that the bank has the right activities and functions to measure and has set reasonable standards, this category evaluates the success of its efforts over time. The quality standards must be based on the expectations of the *customer*. Here's an example of quality gone wrong: During a mid-size Midwestern bank's Quality Council meeting one day, the head of loan operations proudly announced that he had reduced the time it took to deliver statements to customers by a full week. He had hired temporary help, instructed data-processing to run the computers around the clock, and decided to send the statements first-class. There had been an increase in the number that were wrong, but the majority were being delivered correctly and within three business days.

"Is that what our customers want?" asked the manager of the credit department.

"Well . . . ," the answer came, "we really didn't ask them."

After a telephone survey, it was determined that the customers didn't expect their statements until the tenth business day, which meant that there could be more care in producing them and less cost.

Recently, IBM has advertised, "Before we could satisfy the Baldrige Quality Award judges we had to please an even more demanding panel of experts. Our AS/400 customers."[16]

For every product, service, and process, the bank must address error rates, numbers of rejects, account turnover, employee turnover, accuracy of reports and statements, timeliness of introduction and market acceptance, and resource utilization. When these activities are quantified, measurements of the quality results will allow Value Creation and Value Added Teams to identify problems in the structure and the delivery systems and to take the necessary corrective actions, including any that are applicable to suppliers from outside the bank.

Deming argues that the organization should work with one supplier for each particular good or service, involving that vendor in the design phase of the end product, making sure that the organization's quality standards are well understood. Then, working together, in a team situation, the overall quality of the product improves and cost decreases.[17]

The Baldrige Award examines supplier quality, both current and over time, and compares it against other suppliers of the same goods and services. The implication for the bank is that it will have to set quality standards for its vendor support and measure actual results against them. Those that can't measure up may be dropped from the approved vendor list.

"After winning [the Baldrige] in 1988, Motorola told 3,600 of its largest suppliers that they too must be prepared to compete— or else. Two hundred refuseniks have been dropped."[18] Motorola was also one of the companies that was included in a May 1991 report of the General Accounting Office titled "U.S. Companies Improve Performance Through Quality Efforts." This was the first document that contained any historical data about quality improvement in the United States. It was compiled from the numbers of the companies that were among the highest scoring applicants for the Baldrige Award from 1988 to 1990.

Of the 14 companies responding to the questions about the cost of quality, *all of them reported cost savings and improved quality of their products after making the commitment to excellence.* The report contained other dramatic and exciting results:

- Reliability of products and services improved 11.3 percent on average.
- Timeliness of delivery of products increased 4.7 percent.
- Order-processing time was reduced 12 percent.
- The average reduction in defects and errors was 10.3 percent.
- Product lead time was shortened 5.8 percent.
- Inventory turnover rates increased by 7.2 percent.
- The cost of quality was reduced by 9 percent.
- Cost savings from employee suggestions ranged from $1.3 million to $116 million annually.

Considering these tangible results, it seems clear that improving quality and focusing on the customer, increasing share and decreasing cost, are the only strategic objectives to have, even if they are longer-term in nature. Quality Value Engineering does just that, concentrating on the expectations of customers, designing more efficient delivery systems, reorganizing the bank around the new quality orientation, and improving financial performance.

Customer Satisfaction (300 points)

The Baldrige process allocates fully 30 percent of the total number of points to this most important examination category.

First, the company has to define the market segments it serves and the ways to obtain information about them. The Baldrige process evaluates both the choice of markets and the research function. It tests the data-gathering process to see if it is consistent with the company's stated research strategy. Then, it reviews how the company continually improves the entire survey process of defining expectations.

Along with market share data, the bank must determine the satisfaction levels of its customers using service quality surveys such as those presented in Chapter 5. As the bank gathers information about the expectations and perceptions of its customers, it can take positive action to eliminate the gaps between them. This is the type of activity Baldrige examiners want to see. They review survey responses to evaluate the trends with respect to individual and collective customer groups.

Customers set the service standards based on the feedback the bank has obtained from them. If standing in the teller line for ten minutes is too long in the opinion of customers, there must be a resulting action that allows them to accomplish their transactions in less than ten minutes. The award looks at what the standards are and how they were established to insure that the demands of the customers were considered.

This section also examines how the bank treats its customer contact personnel. It looks at the selection process and the training that follows; empowerment and the ability to make customer-related decisions; the reward mechanisms that are in place; career path planning; reasons for turnover; and the adequacy of technology and other tools. It is unfortunate that most financial institutions have not applied these concepts to the tellers and other front-line personnel, since they are the most important people in the organization in the eyes of the customer.

Customer complaints must be documented and acted on to improve service as well. Many companies do not catalog customer problems, but if the customer takes the time to register a complaint, the company had better listen. Procter & Gamble puts an 800 number on its products and encourages customers to call with feedback. They use the information that their customers supply to identify the root cause of problems, which can then be turned into advantage once they are corrected. Customers see that the perceived problem has been corrected and become loyal repeat buyers.

As always, the bank has to provide comparisons of satisfaction levels with its principal competitors. The issues of customer retention, gains and losses in numbers of accounts, and increases and decreases in market share are examples of how the Baldrige examiners determine customer satisfaction. If the company has been recognized by some independent organization for its overall quality and dedication to customer service, those awards would be considered in this category.

THE EXAMINATION PROCESS CONTINUES

The process is tough, rigorous, and leaves nothing to chance. There are those that say that the United States doesn't need a national quality award, especially as part of the federal bureaucracy, and that standards like ISO (International Standards Organization) suffice. The country needs a focus, a lightning rod; standards need to be developed; and the Baldrige Award is achieving those objectives.

The Baldrige guidelines provide any company with a detailed framework with which to build product and service quality. It has prompted American business to improve quality as nothing else has, at a time when it was needed badly.

The quality of the banks' service can increase if they pay attention to the Baldrige guidelines. If the quality improvement process is managed correctly, using the Baldrige for guidance, banks can provide better service. Whether the company wants to apply is a matter of individual choice. But as quality improves, market share will increase, creating real value for the bank, its employees, shareholders, and customers.

> Right now U.S. business is coalescing around the Baldrige as the definitive approach. Mead D'Amore, the general manager of the Commercial Nuclear Fuel Division at Westinghouse which won in 1988, echoes what a lot of senior executives believe: "The Baldrige award has the best set of guidelines I have ever seen." If IBM, Milliken, Westinghouse, and many other companies are using the Baldrige as an internal measure, then clearly it is catching on.[19]

Recently the issue has arisen of companies who pursue winning for winning's sake rather than earnestly wanting to improve quality. The scope of the criteria precludes that possibility. It seems extremely unlikely that a company could make sufficiently substantial changes, as opposed to merely cosmetic, that could withstand the rigorous review process without having a deep commitment to quality for its own sake. Many companies known for top-notch quality haven't applied for the award and do not plan to do so. They just continue to improve the way they service their customers. The Baldrige Award concepts can serve as a guide or a goal, or both, as the bank begins its quality journey.

APPLYING FOR THE BALDRIGE

Once a bank makes the decision to apply for the Baldrige, the examination process begins in earnest. As might be expected, this process becomes increasingly more stringent the farther along an applicant is. The initial examination of the seven categories is known as the first-stage review. In this phase, at least four examiners review the written application, and a panel of judges decides which of the applicants should proceed to the next level of examination, the consensus review.

The purpose of the consensus review is to make the field even smaller. The outcome of it is the list of applicants that will receive a site visit from the examining staff. In this phase, the examiners individually grade each of the applicants and then have dialogue about them, coming to agreement as to where the site visits will occur. There is no magic number of points that qualifies a company for that visit. When they find a company that they think is deserving, the number of points recorded by that company then becomes the cutoff, and all companies receiving the same or a higher number are automatically included on this select list.

For the 1990 award, the total distribution of written scores followed a typical curve, with no applicants in the highest and lowest ranges, and the majority grouped in the middle:

Range%	Applicants in Range
0–125	0%
126–250	7.2%
251–400	18.6%
401–600	52.6%
601–750	19.6%
751–875	2.1%
876–1000	0%

If the company is chosen for a site visit, it is doing very well. The purpose of the site visit is to verify everything that has been documented in the written application and to resolve any questions that have come up during the earlier review stages. It also provides an ideal time for the five members of the board of examiners and the senior examiner to get a feel for the company's quality culture and climate. Those aren't things that they can decipher from a written report.

The site visit is an orderly, mutually arranged process; the examiners provide lists of corporate officials to be interviewed and documents to be prepared for review. The company to be visited is given two weeks' notice and is asked to prepare introductory and concluding presentations of pertinent materials. Typically, these visits are scheduled for the month of September, after which the panel of judges makes its recommendations to NIST, which in turn submits them to the secretary of commerce for the final decisions.

The award ceremony occurs at the White House in October or November. But the Baldrige process does not stop at the end of the first-stage review, consensus review, site visit, or award ceremony. In fact, it never stops. Each applicant receives a report card in the form of the feedback report, which can become the basis for the quality plan for the coming year. These reports are prepared by the examination staff to indicate where the company fell short in each of the examination categories, in order to help the company get better.

> The feedback Milliken got in 1988 helped it win in 1989. Says Roger Milliken, "They told us we didn't have enough objectives." The company adopted a "10-4" goal meaning a tenfold improvement in its quality indexes in four years, by 1993. Milliken observes: "You've got to shoot for objectives that stretch you because then you force everyone to find a new way and not just do it a little bit better." The first year's examiners also found that Milliken's top executives didn't understand statistical process controls well enough. Everybody took a four-day course before the company tried again.[20]

Wayne Cassatt and Ann Rothgeb of the Baldrige Award administration staff believe that most banks simply are not ready to win the award since they have not accumulated enough data. However, at least three are serious about service quality and the Baldrige Award: BancOne, First Tennessee, and MBNA America.

BANCONE

BancOne Corporation has applied for the award twice and has yet to be eligible for a site visit. BancOne's objective in applying is to see how they rank in service quality in comparison to world-class competition. They are educating, setting performance goals, managing, and measuring for quality, across a company that has locations all over the Midwest and in Texas.

The corporation stages an annual internal quality competition among the affiliate banks with the winner being the institution that is allowed to apply. Margaret Kerns, chief quality officer of BancOne—Dayton (Ohio), the bank that won the competition in 1990, told us that the application process took six weeks, and probably should have taken a lot longer. She said that the process itself did nothing to improve the quality of the bank, but it did improve their understanding and perception of what it means to have the total commitment to it.

The most telling comment in that entire conversation occurred when she wondered what would have happened if they had won. She expressed real concern that they might have relaxed and rested on their accomplishment at a time when, in her mind, they still have so much more to do. The more you improve, she said, the more that you see has to be done.

Quality training is emphasized at BancOne. As of early 1991, they had educated over 10,000 people. As the corporation continues to grow by acquisition, the population requiring education increases, which makes Chuck Aubrey's job as chief quality officer that much more difficult. "We teach people that if something is wrong, there's a very high cost to the organization, both in hard and soft dollars."[21] They are encouraged to make the correction as fast as they can with as little customer impact as possible.

FIRST TENNESSEE

When First Tennessee, according to Bob Vezina and Rod White, first learned about the Baldrige in a *USA Today* article, the bank thought it would be a good opportunity to use the criteria for a self-assessment of their quality program. The bank had incorporated quality as a strategic focus and had been using techniques like SPC in their back office since the early 1980s.

The application process at First Tennessee consumed five intense weeks. They established task forces to address each of the seven sections in the application guidelines. The task forces were required to submit daily progress reports, which were studied by a review team charged with approving the final application. As with BancOne, First Tennessee did not receive a site visit. But, they said, the process is worth it, and they would recommend that any bank that has a well-developed quality program at least go through a self-assessment as a preview to an actual application.

They do caution that if the decision is made to undertake it, be prepared for a difficult time. The nature of the bank, with its back-office structure serving many different business units, and the branch network having to sell and service so many different products and customers, makes measurement quite hard. Understand, however, that First Tennessee applied the first year the award existed, a remarkable undertaking in itself. At that time the application was strongly geared to manufacturing companies, although it is much more applicable to service companies now.

First Tennessee has institutionalized the commitment to excellent service quality. It has become the "way things are done around here," and, as such, it is handled as routine. Putting the customer first is the way First Tennessee people do their jobs everyday.

MBNA AMERICA

MBNA America received a site visit from the Baldrige examiners in 1990. From the landscaping, to the attentiveness to their visitors, to the service they provide their customers, to the food in the cafeteria, it is clear that this bank is totally committed to absolute excellence.

The importance of delivering quality service to customers is emphasized throughout the company—from the vice chairman's office to the front-line people in the customer service and credit areas. They put the customer first.

It's always been that way at MBNA America. In fact, they told us that the word "quality" wasn't used until they became involved with the Baldrige Award. They have always determined customer expectations and designed services with them in mind.

If banks aren't careful, there may not be a need for them. The real challenge is service. Every service that the banks offer is also provided by another kind of financial institution; the banks are in a brand new environment.

The banker's world has changed. Quality service, a focus on the customer, a dynamic and responsive organization are the keys to success. Every banker who is reading this book, please call Malcolm Baldrige National Quality Award, 1-301-975-2036, and order copies of the application guidelines.

NOTES

1. Jeremy Main, "How to Win the Baldrige Award," *Fortune*, April 23, 1990, p. 101.

2. Ibid., p. 112.

3. Keith Brinksman, "Banking and the Baldrige (sic) Award," *Bank Marketing*, April 1991, pp. 31–32.

4. Interview with Jack J. Kucler, Senior Vice President, Society Corp., March 12, 1991.

5. Interview with Wayne Cassatt and Ann Rothgeb, National Institute of Standards and Technology, Gaithersburg, Maryland, May 6, 1991.

6. Interview with Shane Flynn, senior vice president, MBNA America, Newark, Delaware, May 7, 1991.

7. "1991 Application Guidelines: The Malcolm Baldrige National Quality Award," p. 7; emphasis added.

8. William A. Band, *Creating Value for Customers* (New York: John Wiley and Sons, 1991), p. 269.

9. Discussion with Douglas L. Hawthorne, CEO, Society Bank, N.A., Dayton, Ohio, March 1987.

10. Interview with Charles Aubrey, chief quality officer, BancOne Corporation, Columbus, Ohio, February 4, 1991.

11. "Cadillac Application Summary," Cadillac Motor Car Company, 1990, p. 3.

12. Curt W. Reimann, "Winning Strategies for The Malcolm Baldrige Award," *Journal of Quality Management*, July 1990, p. 11.

13. Interview with Robert P. Lias, vice president, BancOne, Cleveland, Cleveland, Ohio, February 26, 1991.

14. Marion Horton, "Wallace Goes for the Baldrige," *Supply House Times*, October 1990, p. 248.

15. Reimann, "Winning Strategies for The Malcolm Baldrige Award," p. 16.

16. *Business Week*, December 31, 1990, p. 132.

17. Mary Walton, *The Deming Management Method* (New York: Perigree Books, 1986), p. 64.

18. Main, "How to Win the Baldrige Award," p. 101.

19. Ibid., p. 116.

20. Ibid., p. 112.

21. Interview with Charles Aubrey, chief quality officer, BancOne Corporation, Columbus, Ohio, February 4, 1991.

Chapter 9

The Beginning

We have suggested that Quality Value Engineering benefits the bank's customers, its markets, its employees, and its shareholders. Yet it requires some profound change.

The change that is needed is fundamental, one of attitude and core belief. It is one that says that the old ways of doing things just won't work anymore. Structure, style, and systems are the basis for the paradigms that preclude quality and customer service, with the organization itself the primary culprit. The banks have to focus on their customers; they have to provide quality service; and, most important, they have to restructure their organizations, the activities they undertake, and the way they conduct the business.

Quality Value Engineering allows that to happen. With data and through dialogue, QVE combines a focus on the customer; delivery of high-quality services; and a reconfigured, flattened, and inverted organization structure, all of which lead to improved financial performance.

Improved quality results in lower cost; lower cost provides greater pricing flexibility; high quality with pricing flexibility attracts more customers; a greater number of customers means more transactions; more transactions means a higher margin and fees over which to spread cost; higher earnings provide better ROA and ROE, which result in increased stock price. Quality, quite simply, means profitability and creation of value for the firm.

The nonfinancial benefits are meaningful as well. QVE

means creating an environment of trust and self-esteem, where people can take pride in their work and can be successful. It allows them to participate in creating solutions to problems and rewards them for doing so. It lets them serve their customers, whether internal or external, in a positive atmosphere where they can innovate and have fun.

INSTABILITY RULES

As banks try to shore up their earnings, total quality is the only solution to their problems. In the 1970s and 1980s, their worlds changed dramatically and rapidly. Instability rules the industry, and they are not prepared for it. They maintain traditional policies and procedures; their organization structures remain as they have been for 50 years; and their ways of handling customers continue, even as the environment in which they exist becomes completely different.

The reasons for the unstable conditions are many. Improved technology creates a smaller and faster financial marketplace for all banks, not just Chase Manhattan and the money center banks that send funds all over the world. They have to automate to compete, but it costs them more and does not necessarily provide the anticipated productivity improvements.

The industry is also characterized by failure and loss, triggered by declining real estate values in the Southwest, New England, and California. Losses force interminable cost-cutting. Citicorp cut 5,000 jobs because it lost $400 million on a subsidiary called Quotron. What business does Citicorp think it is in? How do banking people relate to this nonbanking subsidiary?

When the problems in the real estate portfolio were discovered at Bank of New England, the response was to cut 5,000 people. What relationship do they have to the credit problems? Don't the people who were displaced at BNE and Citicorp add value to the bank? They must be doing something to service customers, and now that they are gone, service levels decline.

The strategy is to compensate for business losses with staff reductions. Some banks like U.S. Bancorp and First Bank System see that they have potential earnings problems so they simply reduce the workforce by 10 percent. Although it seems like the right thing to do, it does not produce the results that they think it will. The banks reduce their expenses across-the-board and do not consider the value of what they produce from the customer's perspective. As Judy Brooks of J. P. Morgan & Co. asks rhetorically, "What happened to the customers they served? Did they leave the bank? Where did they go?"[1]

Banks are consolidating operations and branches, getting farther and farther away from the customer. The NABCA survey points out that most banks that have undertaken a cost management project have used reduction techniques since these are the only ones they know. Taking out people and undergoing consolidations only hurt customer service. Banking is a people business, a fundamental that many of today's bankers may have forgotten. If the bank is organized properly and the customer is always first in the minds of the staff, this will not have to happen. "Do what you have to do to satisfy the client," says Richard C. Hyde, executive vice president at Ameritrust. "We didn't and look where it got us."[2]

Bankers have always treated the symptoms of the problems instead of getting to their root causes, never considering that the real reasons for the trouble are lodged in the structure and environment of the bank. They watch the price of common shares drop and cut dividends to their shareholders, a short-term gesture. The losses and thinner margins force mergers, even of the biggest banks such as Security Pacific and Bank of America, but the reasons for them—taking advantage of excess capacity and gaining economies of scale—are seldom realized. Cost creep sees to that. Bankers do not consider that their united organizations look exactly the same as before, only bigger. They cut out people within the pyramid and do not do fundamental organization redesign around their products, services, and markets.

As margins are squeezed, the banks look for ways to increase their customer bases; one way is to venture into new geographic markets through acquisitions, hoping to achieve economies that will add to profitability. Key Bank moves from its native New York into Idaho, creating additional competition for West One. SunTrust moves into Florida and Tennessee. BancOne is in Illinois and Texas. Norwest is in Montana, South Dakota, Nebraska, Wisconsin, North Dakota, Indiana, Iowa, and Arizona, in addition to its Minnesota home. This geographic expansion creates additional market opportunities for the invading bank, but also increases competition in these markets, forcing narrower margins.

Competition comes from outside the United States as well. The list of the largest banks in the world no longer contains any American banks. Banks from France, Japan, England, Germany, and others are represented in New York or Los Angeles, in the biggest and newest office buildings. The financial marketplace is global.

AT&T wants credit card business. GMAC finances cars at a rate that the banks can not touch. There are leasing companies everywhere to promote business expansion. The brokerages process incredible numbers of transactions every day as they provide consumers with various investment opportunities. Nonbank banks continue to expand their offerings and encroach deeper and deeper into banks' territory.

With all of this turbulence, one thing is certain. It will continue, creating, paradoxically, a kind of stability. The first time a takeover took place, for example, it was new and different. Now, they are commonplace. The same can be said for cost-cutting projects, better technology, new competition, and geographic expansion. That means that the bankers of the twenty-first century will have to be able to accept change as a matter of fact and to be able to deal with it routinely and effectively.

QUALITY VALUE ENGINEERING CAN HELP

Deming wrote, "I want to make clear that as you improve quality, your costs go down."[3] The cost of quality in America's banks is high—as much as 30 percent of noninterest expense or even higher. Undoubtedly, they are unknowingly paying people to make mistakes. In one company keypunchers knew there was an error on the input documents but continued to enter the transactions into the system, only to have them reject. The bank had to correct the rejected items so it hired people to work in the adjustment department, fixing the symptom, not the real cause. When they fixed this immediate problem, they had to generate a corrected statement or transaction advice, which was then mailed to the customer. Postage was added to the cost of quality. Such wasted time and money seem ludicrous, yet who had the charter to look at the big picture, find the root cause, and fix it? If the bank continues to make mistakes, customers finally say, "That's enough," and go out the back door, taking their deposit balances, loans, credit card fees, overdraft charges, and other fees with them. That causes problems for the people who have to replenish the assets and liabilities that have left, and who have to spend a lot of marketing time and dollars doing it, when they could be pursuing new business.

Mistakes caused by the process design multiply as they get closer to the customer. Banks, however, continue to try to resolve customer problems by correcting problems rather than preventing them. That is where Quality Value Engineering comes in. Using the bank's own best resources and experts—its employees—problems are creatively solved at the root, by analyzing and understanding data that quantify the extent, size, and location of the service quality symptoms and, more important, the organizational issues that underlie them.

Errors are expensive, too; fewer errors mean less waste. Every time there is an error, time has to be spent correcting it, time that could be spent on satisfying customer's financial needs. Misposts on a savings account are not the only errors the bank can have. An error can be something as big as distribution of a new procedure and implementation of a changed system on payday. One bank issued the order to pay the quarterly dividend *twice*. Imagine trying to stop payment on checks issued to shareholders and having to admit that another check was in the mail, and just think of the waste: an extra run of 3 million dividend checks; the time to call shareholders; the letters that had to be sent; time with the transfer agent; changing the transfer agent; and so on.

With fewer mistakes and rework, the bank has more time to concentrate on its customers, internal as well as external. There is much unnecessary effort expended in the bank that could be directed toward improvement:

- preparing reports that nobody reads, simply because it has always been done
- attending meetings that hash the same things over and over again
- following the decision tree where approvals must be obtained higher and higher into the organization when those people hardly realize what they are making a decision about
- putting financial people in line units to take the data prepared by the controller's department and reformatting it to suit their own purposes
- laying off employees in one area and hiring from the outside in another instead of engaging in retraining

If the bank can design the errors out of processes, there will be less finger-pointing and blame being assigned for the mistakes. There will be fewer battles between the branches and deposit operations; calling officers and the credit department; everyone and finance; and a more stable, more trusting environment will result.

And there will be higher demand for its services. Remember, QVE is based on demand side customer service: Find out what customers want, the volumes that they need, and the quality level that will satisfy them, and produce it.

Bank customers have low expectations about the service they receive. But that doesn't square with the fact that ATMs have to be available 24 hours a day; that loan payments have to be recorded accurately; that interest must be computed and paid properly and on a timely basis; or that the right amounts are deducted from checking accounts. Customers question the bank's ability to deliver first-rate service, but that is exactly what they want.

> Consumers increasingly find themselves paying more for service—and liking it less. Frustration over service rivals the public's complaints over poor-quality goods. Hang around your favorite service establishment, and often it's just a matter of time before fingernails tap or tempers flare.[4]

Customers think that dealing with the bank is a hassle, and they are right. If the bank can meet their expectations by raising the level of service it provides, there is significant advantage to be gained.

If the bank is doing the right thing, the right way, the first time and every time, it can organize itself to emphasize sales and service and to eliminate the bureaucracy that characterizes most of them. Banks need to turn their organizations upside down to where the tellers are on the top and are being coached and supported by everyone else. The same holds true for the mortgage loan originators, branch managers, trust officers, and anyone else whose job it is to actually see and service customers. On MBNA America's paychecks are the words, "Brought to you by the Customer."

A lot of the people in the bank never see customers, and even fewer consider the economics of having them. Many employees don't realize that they are all part of a system that puts services into the hands of the public. They don't discern that an extra layer of management results in higher than necessary product costs, or that running that extra report adds to the cost of service. Many do not understand that if they make a mistake in the back office, customers do come into the branch to try to get it resolved, that fingernails do tap and tempers actually flare.

Consider the following telephone conversation:

> I'd like to talk with someone about my account. A mistake has been made, and a transaction was posted incorrectly. I've called

your bank now three times, and all I get is the Voice Mail, and nobody has returned my calls.

I finally got through this afternoon, but the person, and I don't know who it was, couldn't have cared less. He couldn't answer my question and said that some policy wouldn't let him deal with this. Then he told me to call you.

So I did and they put me on hold. For five minutes, nothing. Then it took them another ten minutes to find my account and they didn't understand that the transaction was wrong.

Then they said, 'You mean *that* account? I'll try to find it.' That took another five minutes. What kind of systems do you have? You can't find my account; it's wrong; and it's not related to my other accounts; and you tell me in your advertising that you're reliable!"

This is not uncommon: just ask the people in the customer service department. If the bank can do the transaction properly the first time and every time, this type of thing doesn't happen. The bank ends up with happy customers and the cost of doing business is reduced. And reduced costs lead to increased earnings, pricing elasticity, and even more customers.

As Value Creation and Value Added Teams engage in dialogue, they design errors out of the delivery systems. In doing so, people who have worked in the same bank for years really get to know each other and to understand how what they do affects everyone else. Most people don't understand their interrelationships with their fellow employees and how they fit in the overall delivery of the bank's services. Having them work together to solve common business problems is a very positive experience.

And they have fun! They have targets to work on: service quality gaps, structural impediments, and the 30 percent of expenses that is related to doing things wrong. These give them a focus, something tangible and measurable. Most important of all, they are empowered to do something about it. They can cause change; they can have impact.

It makes the bank a more positive place to work. At MBNA America, "People who like people" is the attitude, and you can feel it the moment you walk through the front door. Helping each other is much more positive than the continual tension at most banks. There is also pride in knowing that the job has been done right, whether it be the landing of a new account, solving a customer's problem, the development of a system, preparation of a plan, or even cutting the grass. That's an internal motivation that says that employees have contributed, in their own way, to the success of the bank.

Most quality problems are caused by the environment at the bank, the structure, and the inability to serve. Quality Value Engineering allows the bank's teams to identify and correct them, creating a positive culture and attitude and improving financial results.

SIX KEY ELEMENTS FOR A SUCCESSFUL JOURNEY

The goal of *Quality Value Banking* has been to give America's bankers a long-term value creation strategy that will have positive results in terms of financial performance. To achieve that, a bank must possess six key elements:

- Unwavering commitment to quality throughout the organization
- A sharp focus on the customer
- A policy of resource reallocation and redeployment
- Continuation of the Dialogue process over the long term
- Willingness to accept the effects of change
- A system to monitor performance and reward excellence

Organizational Commitment

Quality Value Engineering requires a commitment from everyone in the bank to the new quality customer service orientation. Starting at the top of the house, the CEO and the rest of management must demonstrate, from the outset, that quality client service is the bank's only strategy.

The members of the Quality Council must be the champions of service quality. They must have the attitude that when they see an error, they say to the rest of the bank, "This will never happen again," and empower the people to make sure that it doesn't. They must be the examples that nothing is too good for the bank's customers, realizing that once they start down the path to quality, they can never turn back. The challenge then becomes to improve continually, always trying to figure out new ways of delivering even better service. They are the coaches who encourage and motivate the rest of the organization to do even better, reaching higher service quality plateaus.

They must be totally dissatisfied with the complacency that has ruled many banks. Because the banks were regulated for so long, practices and procedures were established that were based on a stable marketplace. But instability has become the only kind of stability the banking industry can rely on. In the words of General Electric executive John Trani, "Change is never easy when you do it on multiple fronts. But the organization that adapts itself continually will win and for that you have to have leaders and managers who love change."[5]

Education, communication, and participation are the keys. Management must understand what the commitment to quality means and that enthusiasm must be shared with the rest of the employees. There must be continual training about the quality customer service orientation in workshops, in the Value Creation and Value Added Teams, and on the job. Communication all across the bank about the processes under study and the results that are being achieved must occur constantly and consistently. As one CEO said, "There are 4,000 people in the bank. We want each of them to think about the best ways to service our customers."

All bank employees must develop a curiosity about the way the bank delivers those services to its customers and devise creative and innovative solutions to problems that the bank may not have realized it had. As such, Quality Value Engineering depends on the dedication of the Value Creation and Value Added Teams to engage in true dialogue to solve them. Patience with each other and with the process is essential. Improved quality won't happen overnight, so employees must resolve to work together for however long it takes to get there.

Focus on the Customer

There is no question that improved quality leads to better customer service as well as to reduced cost. The bank will attract and keep more customers because it has higher-quality products. Quality professionals and others have long believed this to be true, and the General Accounting Office report proved it.

The bank improves quality by developing data to identify where the service problems are and then rearranging the delivery system to eliminate them, producing zero defects. It also improves quality by creating a structure that is directed at serving customers and eliminates unnecessary activities.

Through statistical analyses, the expectations and perceptions of customers across the five dimensions of service quality—reliability, responsiveness, assurance, tangibles, and empathy—must be calculated, computing the gaps between them. In this way, a bank knows what customers want, what they think they are getting, and how important it is to them. Then all the bank has to do is organize itself and its delivery system to provide it. A focused, customer-oriented delivery system and elimination of unnecessary activities provide a better overall environment in which to work, which also contributes to better service.

Servicing customers is more fun than hearing their complaints. All that the bank does is provide service, which Webster defines as "benefit, advantage, and friendly help." If the bank makes the experience of coming to the bank pleasant, customers will come back, and maybe they will tell their friends, and the whole economic cycle will begin again.

Reallocation of Resources

There is another positive feature of QVE that encourages participation: resource reallocation or redeployment. Whenever the subject of savings targets comes up, bankers always think that it will result in people losing their jobs. The objective of QVE is to minimize that. There is the possibility of some displacement. But the differentiating characteristic of QVE is the talent bank into which valuable resources can be invested and from which the bank can withdraw to reinvest elsewhere, given the proper education.

If the Value Creation and Value Added Teams know that the talent bank is operating, there is a more positive motivation for them than if it were not. QVE may ask employees to assume new duties, but the goal is for no one to lose a job because of it. The issue of resource reallocation must be addressed at the outset of QVE by the CEO. It is the first critical decision that must be made, and the bank must commit to it before there is any contact with the employees in order to avoid rumors and speculation. The CEO needs to assure the employees that the bank is actually engaging in resource reallocation, not downsizing and displacement. Members of the Quality Council and the QVE facilitators must echo that policy in all of their communication and then live up to the promise.

Continue the Dialogues

The job of the Value Creation Team members really begins when their series of Dialogues is over. They will lead and participate on other teams, but more important, they will make sure that the improvements they recommend are implemented, and then they will work together to continually improve their organization and delivery system.

Service quality surveys should be conducted annually to gauge that performance as well as to see if customer expectations have changed. Customer requirements and markets may become different, and the bank must know this and capitalize on it. The team environment, with rotating membership, permits open and honest dialogue to learn those customer requirements and design processes to satisfy them.

Team membership does need to change. On a regular basis, different people should become part of the team to acquaint them with Quality Value Engineering, to tackle new problems, and to bring a fresh perspective to old problems. The more people the bank has that are involved with the quality and customer orientation, the better.

Organizational Effects

Employees need to know that the bank is committed to delivering first-rate service to both internal and external customers and what that means for them. Everyone must understand that QVE asks them to perform at a higher level every day, but that processes have been redesigned to make their lives easier. There will be standards for them to achieve, but working together as a team, all of them will be aiming for the same goals and objectives.

They will see the bank change organizationally with fellow employees being asked to take on new assignments and responsibilities. There may be fewer people in the department since they won't have as many mistakes to correct; they may end up reporting within a structure that is different; and they may find themselves being trained for something that is completely different than what they were doing before.

They will see a change in what is being asked of them, as well. QVE fosters participation and empowerment, which will alter the way they do their jobs. With a minimum of rules and controls, they are encouraged to do whatever it takes to satisfy customer requirements. "Capable workers who are well trained and fairly compensated provide better service, need less supervision, and are much more likely to stay on the job."[6]

More customers mean more profits; high quality equates to low cost. Together, these provide two advantages in the marketplace. First, customers will use the bank that has high-quality services. Second, the bank can gain a pricing advantage, charging less than its competition and still increasing the per item contribution to net income. Higher quality and a competitive price can't be beat.

As earnings increase, the ratios that the analysts use also improve. They see the strength of the bank and the stock becomes a good investment. Of course, more demand for a product will drive the price up, providing additional value for the shareholder. That higher stock price allows the bank to remain independent since others will not be able to afford to buy it, or should it decide to sell, it can command a premium from the buyer, enriching the shareholders even more.

Monitor Performance/Reward Employees

A strong motivation for participation is the recognition of those who have contributed to the bank's success. Recognition can be in the form of monetary rewards or nonfinancial appreciation. A very simple method is to put the names of the people who have worked on a VCT or a VAT in the bank's monthly newsletter. Another is to have a recognition banquet in which the team members are identified by the CEO as having made that contribution. There are other ways, but whatever form they take, recognition and reward must be genuine. Nothing will kill QVE faster than superficial support throughout the process and artificial rewards.

As with everything in QVE, the reward system must be based on data. Smaller things like putting names in the paper or awarding a coffee mug may be done without it, but for the reward system to work, the bank has to have results. It will require a different look at financial information to take the guesswork out of rewarding the participants. The teams must create systems that will allow that quantification to occur. The cost of quality, identified early in the process, becomes the target for the teams. The system will be required to track the impacts of the recommendations to eliminate unnecessary activities and to reallocate resources, providing comparisons against the targets to gauge the potential improvement. As implementation occurs, it must account for the actual results, comparing them against the plans. These results become the basis for the rewards.

Recognition is one of the most powerful motivating tools. It shows people that the company cares about them and what they have done. It provides them with a feeling of self-worth and creates an environment where they want to contribute to the success of the team.

The Beginning

At this point in most books, the authors are winding down, drawing conclusions, and summarizing what they have written. This last chapter does a little of that, but more important, it encourages America's bankers to start their own journeys to quality.

Quality Value Engineering is a detailed, thoughtful, comprehensive, yet essentially simple methodology to improve the quality of products, services, operations, and customer relations. It is based on the quality research of the last 50 years. QVE applies it to banks, concentrating on improving market share and reducing the cost of providing service.

This book has demonstrated how Quality Value Engineering works, the reasons that the banks have gotten into the mess that they are in, and some of the "slash-and-burn" methods they have used in the attempt to get out. It has also shown that these methods do not work in the long run and that a focus on customers and a redesign of the organization to provide quality service is the only successful strategy.

Although this is the end of *Quality Value Banking* (the book), may it be the beginning of quality value banking in your bank.

NOTES

1. Interview with Judy Brooks, vice president, J. P. Morgan & Co., January 6, 1992.

2. Interview with Richard C. Hyde, executive vice president, Ameritrust Co., N. A., October 17, 1991.

3. Mary Walton, *The Deming Management Method* (New York: Perigee Books, 1986), p. 26.

4. Joan Berger, "In the Service Sector, Nothing is 'Free' Anymore," *Business Week,* June 8, 1987, p. 144.

5. John Huey, "Nothing Is Impossible," *Fortune,* September 23, 1991, p. 139.

6. Leonard A. Schlesinger and James L. Heskett, "The Service-Driven Service Company," *Harvard Business Review,* September–October 1991, p. 72.

Glossary

ABCA   activity-based cost accounting

Administrivia   the myriad of little things that take people away from the primary focus of their responsibilities

ATA   automation/technology analysis

ATMs   automatic teller machines

AVP   assistant vice president

Benchmarking   determination of the standards from which improvements will be made

CDs   certificates of deposit

CEO   chief executive officer

Chain of command   a series of vertical reporting relationships

Closing the back door   having service so good that customers do not close their accounts

CMA   cash management account

Concurrent engineering   involving customers, suppliers, and representatives from the affected areas of the bank in product design

Cost creep   reappearance of expenses relating to activities deemed to be of value by customers

Cost drivers   the reasons expenses are incurred

Cost of poor quality   the expenses that would not be incurred if everything were perfect

CQO   chief quality officer

Culture   the ways things are done

Customer service   conforming to requirements with zero defects, within acceptable limits of variation

CWQC   company-wide quality control

Deming chain reaction providing more jobs by improving quality, which decreases costs, increases productivity, and results in greater market share

Demystifying sharing heretofore corporate secrets

Dialogue free flow of meaning between people

DIDMCA Depository Institutions Deregulation and Monetary Control Act of 1980

DIRFT "Do it right the first time"

DIRST "Do it right the second time"

Diversification spreading the loan portfolio across many industries and geographic areas

Eurodollars U.S. dollars traded with European banks

EVP executive vice president

FDIC Federal Deposit Insurance Corporation

Flowchart a graphic representation of a service delivery system or process

FTE full-time equivalent person

Gainsharing sharing the financial benefits of quality increases with employees

GMAC General Motors Acceptance Corporation

HLTs highly leveraged transactions

IRA individual retirement account

ISO International Standards Organization

Juran Trilogy quality planning, quality control, and quality improvement

Knowledge preservation documenting and storing information for use by subsequent groups

Knowledge transfer the ability of one group to learn from another

LDC loans to developing countries

Macro-organization the overall management and functional structure of an organization as distinct from the structure of an individual area, process, or program

MBA Masters Degree of Business Administration

MBO   management by objective

MCIF   Marketing customer information file

Meganational bank   financial institutions with assets over $250 billion, operating across the country

NABCA   National Association for Bank Cost and Management Accounting

NIE   noninterest expense

NIST   National Institute of Standards and Technology

NOW Accounts   negotiable orders of withdrawal

NSF Check   nonsufficient funds in an account to cover a check

OEA   organization environment analysis

Organization structure   the arrangement in place to divide and coordinate work

PA   performance appraisal

PAM   product and activity measurement

Paradigm   a pattern, model, or example; that is, the way it's always been done

PC   personal computer

PIMS   Profit Impact of Market Strategies

Process diagramming   drawing a service delivery system based on customer quality expectations

Quality Value Engineering   determining customer demand and required quality levels, reorganizing the delivery system to provide the expected service

QVE   Quality Value Engineering

Refuseniks   suppliers that do not adhere to the quality standards of their customers

Resource redeployment   taking excess human capacity from an area where customer demand has slackened, retraining them, and reallocating them to areas where demand is high

REITs   real estate investment trusts

RIF   reduction-in-force

ROA   return on assets

ROE   return on equity

ROI   return on investment

Root causes the underlying and fundamental reasons for problems and poor service quality

Service delivery system all of the activities involved in providing a given service to a customer

Slash-and-burn indiscriminate cost cutting

Span of control the number of people overseen by a supervisor or manager

SPC statistical process control

SQM service quality measurement

Statementing preparing customer statements

Statistical process control measuring the variations in a process sufficiently to result in a stable state

SVP senior vice president

Survivor syndrome syndrome experienced by those employees remaining after a cost-cutting program or merger, characterized by fear of making mistakes and not taking risks

Talent bank a methodology or process for resource redeployment

Title inflation proliferation of names identifying corporate ranking

TRIPROL Joseph Juran's triple role: everyone is a customer, a processor, and a supplier

Unity of purpose cooperation toward a single goal

VATs Value Added Teams

VCTs Value Creation Teams

Zero defects no errors or mistakes; a quality goal popularized by Philip Crosby in *Quality Is Free*

Index

Activity-based cost accounting system, 191
American Express, 26, 28
American Savings Bank, 121
Ameritrust, 24, 210
AT&T, 26, 191, 211
Aubrey, Charles, 61, 179, 196, 204

Baldrige, Malcolm, 182
Baldrige Award. *See* Malcolm Baldrige National Quality Award
BancOne, 28, 211
BankOne-Cleveland, 193
BankOne-Dayton, 204
Bank of America, 7, 27
Bank of Boston, 24
Bank of New England, 23, 24, 209
Bank of New York, 23
Bank of North Dakota, 42
Banking
    basics of, 29–30
Banking Act of 1935, 34–36
Bannerman, W. Douglas, 42
Barnett Banks, 24
Becker, Otto, 46
Bell Laboratories, 53, 54
Benchmarks, 2, 143, 148, 159, 164, 169, 171, 173, 177, 179, 189, 191
Bennett, David, ix
Berry, Leonard M., ix, 61, 79
Boston Celtics, 161
Brooks, Judy, 210
Brown, Carter, ix
Bush, George, 183

Cadillac Motor Car Division, 181, 184, 192
Canon, 191
Capital-to-asset ratio, 43
Cash management account (CMA), 38–39, 42
Cassatt, Wayne, 189, 203

Cawley, Charles, 69, 189
Certificate of deposit (CD), 36–37
Chase Manhattan Bank, 24, 28, 209
Citicorp, 7, 24, 27, 36, 191, 209
C&S, 24
C&S/Sovran, 23
Commercial paper, 37
Comptroller of the Currency, 35
Continental Illinois, 23
Cormack, David, 167
Cornell, Bonnie, 95
Corning, 186
Corporate titles, 12–14
"Cost creep," 46, 210
Cost cutting, 44
Cost drivers, 84–87
Cost management survey, 47–50, 70, 88
Crestar Bank, 81
Crosby, Philip, ix, 53, 55, 60, 79, 81, 128
Cummins Engine, 186
Cycle of stability, 6

D'Amore, Mead, 201
Deming, W. Edwards, ix, 53, 54, 79, 194, 197, 211
    and statistical process control, 56–59, 116
Deming Prize, 55, 185
Depository Institutions Deregulation and Monetary Control Act of 1980 (DIDMCA), 23, 40–41
Detoy, Richard, 99
Dialogue, 159–160, 162
Digital Equipment Corporation (DEC), 191
Discover Card, 26
Diversification, 29–30
Dividends
    suspension and elimination of, 43
Downward spiral, 6

E. F. Hutton, 38
Elorriaga, John, 45
Ernst & Young, 47–50
Eurodollars, 37–38

FDIC, 23, 24, 33, 35, 36
Federal Express Corporation, 49, 72,
    183, 184
Federal Reserve System, 35, 191
Feigenbaum, Armand, ix
Fifth Discipline, The, ix, 159
First Bank System, 44, 210
First Chicago, 24, 186
First Interstate Bank Ltd., 28, 44
First Interstate Bank of California, 181
First of America, 28
First Wachovia, 28
Flatbush National Bank, 26
Fleet/Norstar, 24, 44
Ford Motor Company, 191

Garn–St. Germain Act, 23, 41
Geneen, Harold S., 60
General Accounting Office, 198, 218
General Electric, 217
General Electric Capital Corporation,
    26
General Motors Acceptance Corpora-
    tion, 26, 28, 211
Glass, Carter, 33
Glass–Steagall Act, 23, 33–36, 42
Globe Metallurgical, 184, 185
Goldman, Sachs, 38
Great Depression, 31, 33–35
GTE Telephone, 186

Hamada, Hiroshi, 86
Hanick, David S., 30
Hay point system, 4
Holub, Aleta, 186
Hostile takeovers, 23
Huntington Bancshares, 23
Hyde, Richard C., 210

IBM, 191, 197, 201
IBM-Rochester, 184
International Standards Organization
    (ISO), 200
Irving Trust Company, 23

John Deere, 191
J. P. Morgan Company, 32, 210

Juran, Joseph, ix, 53, 55, 59, 78, 80, 81,
    116

Kerns, Margaret, 204
KeyBanks, 28, 211
Kucler, Jack, 186

L. L. Bean, 186, 191
Leach, Ken, 185
Lias, Bob, 193
Livengood, Earl, 45
Los Angeles Times, 10

McCoy, John, 67
McFadden Act of 1927, 23
Main, Jeremy, 183
Malcolm Baldrige National Quality
    Award, 53, 67, 71–73, 81, 116, 156,
    164, 178, 181–206
    application for, 201–203
    key concepts of, 187
Marlow Industries, 184
MBNA America, 26, 72, 156
Medlin, John G., Jr., 61
Mellon Bank, 24
Mergers
    Manufacturers Hanover/Chemical
        Bank, 28
    Security Pacific/Bank of America,
        28, 210
Merrill Lynch, 7, 38, 42
Milliken & Company, 116, 184, 201, 203
MNC Financial, 24
"Moments of truth," 175
Morrison, Bill, 69
Motorola, Inc., 184, 185, 192, 197

National Association for Bank Cost
    and Management Accounting
    (NABCA), 47–50, 70, 88, 181, 210
National Institute of Standards and
    Technology (NIST), 72, 182, 193
NationsBank, 23
NBD, 28
NCNB, 23, 24
Nelson, Lloyd, 59
Next, 186
New Hope Communication, 70
Norwest, 211

Organization
    as foundation for service quality, 1